Teaching Creative Writing:
Practical Approaches

Edited by Elaine Walker PhD

Imprint information
and credits

978-1-907076-47-3 (Paperback edition)
978-1-907076-12-1 (Hardback edition)

Published under the Creative Writing Studies imprint by
The Professional and Higher Partnership Ltd
Registered office: Suite 7 Lyndon House, 8 King's Court,
Willie Snaith Road, Newmarket, Suffolk, CB8 7SG, UK

Imprint website: creativewritingstudies.wordpress.com
Company website: http://pandhp.com

First published 2012
© Elaine Walker and contributors

Credits
Cover image: Rika Newcombe (www.rikanewcombe.co.uk)
Cover design, text design and typesetting: Benn Linfield
    (www.bennlinfield.com)
Copy-editing: Karen Haynes
Index: Christina Garbutt
Proofreading: Richard Kitchen

Disclaimer

The Professional and Higher Partnership Ltd has no responsibility for the persistence or accuracy of URLs for external or third-party websites referred to in this publication, and does not guarantee that any content on such websites is, or will remain, accurate or appropriate.

The material contained in this publication is provided in good faith as general guidance. The advice and strategies contained herein may not be suitable for every situation. No liability can be accepted by The Professional and Higher Partnership Ltd for any liability, loss, risk, or damage which is incurred as a consequence, whether direct or indirect, of using or applying any of the contents of this book or the advice or guidance contained therein.

The publisher and the author make no warranties or representations with respect to the completeness or accuracy of the contents of this work and specifically disclaim all warranties, including without limitation warranties of fitness for a particular purpose. No warranty may be created or extended by sales or promotional materials.

Series information

Teaching creative writing: practical approaches is the second title to be published in the international series, Creative Writing Studies. The series comprises titles on creative writing designed for use – by scholars, students, and teachers – in higher education settings.
The first title of the series was:
Rethinking creative writing in higher education by Stephanie Vanderslice

Further titles commissioned for the series include:
Creative writing: writers on writing, edited by Amal Chatterjee
Researching creative writing by Jen Webb
Studying creative writing, edited by Sharon Norris

95   22 Digital lyre: conducting an audio workshop
         Stefanie Wortman

99   23 To You or not to You?: using second person in prose
         Barrie Llewelyn

103 24 The paperless workshop: save trees, increase
         interaction, reduce preciousness
         Steve May

107 25 Put it on a postcard: capturing the poetic moment
         in prose
         Patricia Debney

110 26 Finding a suitable narrative voice when writing for
         children
         Gill James

115 27 Writing with Shakespeare and Montaigne: past
         practices for future writers
         Eric LeMay

120 28 Earth, Air, Fire and Water: a writing and performance
         workshop
         Lisa Samson

124 29 Gift wraps: a collaborative poetry game
         Philip Gross

129 30 Write what you know: fictionalising every day
         experience
         M. Y. Alam

133 31 Structuring the perfect short story: how to create a
         strong plot arc
         Joanna Barnden

137   32   Hands-on activities for experimental drama: crafting and directing spectacles
Will Cordeiro

142   33   Exploring multiple viewpoints to create compelling narratives
Meg Vandermerwe

145   34   Teaching the critical reflective essay
Sharon Norris

149   35   How to write a bad poem
Allene Nichols

154   36   Considering connotation: the impact and implications of language in poetry
Lesley Burt

159   37   Whatever!: exploring the 'authentic voice' in young-adult fiction
Vanessa Harbour

163   38   'Give and take': getting a stage play on its feet
Paul Lucas

167   39   Start where you are: read what you know
Michelle M. Crawford

171   40   Writing suspense(fully)
Michael G. Cornelius

175   41   Other talents: 'doing creative (writing)'
Amy Letter

179   42   Fascinating rhythm: teaching songwriting – a multimodal experience
Sharon Norris

185   43 Leaving the comfort zone: against practicality and
          rationality
          Nicholas Y.B. Wong
189   44 Flights of fancy: writing from myth
          Amina Alyal
193   45 Found poetry workshop
          Colleen Kearney Rich
197   46 30/30 projects: developing a daily writing habit
          Ian Williams
202   47 Using guided walks in creative writing: wandering,
          observing, describing
          Will Cordeiro
207   48 Researching for the fiction writer
          DeMisty D. Bellinger
211   49 Writing with the masters: finding creativity in copying
          Adam Robert Floridia
216   50 Describing with feeling: evoking style, tone and
          emotion in script scene directions
          Craig Batty
221   Afterword: writing outside the book
223   Bibliography
229   Thematic index

Foreword

Creative writing as a university subject is unusual in that it draws its academics from a variety of disciplines. While a historian is likely to have a history background, a writer's career often develops from – and may continue to include – several strands. Therefore, the personal resource brought to the delivery of creative writing courses may differ widely between individual lecturers while being linked by the experience of publication.

The contributors to this book are all published writers as well as experienced lecturers and educators. They include travel, life and food writers, playwrights and lyricists, as well as novelists and poets. They lecture in literature, language, sociology, history and cultural studies as well as creative writing and, while their ideas are gathered together between the pages of this book, they are based across the five continents. As an insight into the creative individual behind each exercise, they are introduced through a variation on the standard academic bio based on the first exercise, which is my own contribution.

While the exercises all follow the same pattern of presentation, they reflect the approach, style and cultural heritage of the individual contributor. Focused on academic rigor and creative flair, they offer eclecticism and innovation alongside original approaches to familiar sticking points for writing students. They are positioned randomly so those who prefer to dip in are not confined by preconceived connections. For those who prefer navigation, however, the thematic index and extension ideas in the afterword are available.

These exercises can be adapted to suit your style and your students or used exactly as written. They are all fully field-tested and ready to feed into your resource collection.

ELAINE WALKER
Editor

1

'Who I am' icebreaker: establishing a group dynamic

Introduction

Icebreakers are a useful starter for group work. Even in a creative writing class without a workshop element, it's likely that the students will be asked to read their work out or share copies with the group. The sense of vulnerability involved can be eased by establishing a comfortable working environment from the outset.

This exercise is one I've adapted from a drama workshop warm-up and I vary it depending on the creative writing course I'm teaching. I find it especially useful with online groups to help give each faceless name an associated identity. In a face-to-face class it can help students move beyond judging by appearances. In both situations, the exercise serves as a leveller and an introduction to each member as an individual.

The exercise

The students are provided with the following pro forma to complete, adapted to suit the class remit.

Who I am

My name is:

My name-story:

My writing:

I recommend that you read this [play/novel/poetry]:

My favourite [poem/minor character/stage direction/ line from a play/opening to a novel, depending on the focus of the course]:

Ask me if you need information on:

I can't help you with:

You'd never have known if I hadn't told you that:

Mixing standard personal information headings with more unexpected ones works well. For example, if asked for a memorable stage direction, rather than simply a favourite play, the students have to think a little more deeply and the replies often lead to further discussion and interaction.

Questions can be varied according to the make-up of the group. For example, with an online group that I know has members who are under eighteen or well into retirement, I'd include a question that revealed this information without asking students to give their age. This can help establish appropriate boundaries of language and content at an early stage.

STARTING THE EXERCISE WITH ONLINE GROUPS

In an online group, I post the pro forma to the forum, followed by my own completed example. This introduces me to the group and offers a model for anyone who is unsure what's wanted.

STARTING THE EXERCISE FACE TO FACE

In a face-to-face class, I provide copies of the pro forma and ask the group to work in pairs, giving the information to their partner to note down. I make up one of the pairs or, with an even number group, give my own information as an example.

WORKING ONLINE

When I post the pro forma, I ask the students to greet one another and ask for brief further information on each bio as it is submitted. In a very large group, I ask them to respond to only two or three fellow students and to make their choices so as to balance numbers of queries and responses as far as possible.

I allow about a week for this exercise during an asynchronous online class before moving on, but then leave it open throughout the remainder of the course. Latecomers are encouraged to complete the exercise and existing members to go back and welcome them.

WORKING FACE TO FACE

Once each pair has exchanged information, I ask the students to introduce their partner to the group based on what they have learned. Alternatively, I may ask them to write and read out a publicity blurb which 'bigs up' their partner in good Hollywood million-seller novel style.

Getting the group to laugh with – never at – one another is the best icebreaker there is and this can lead to a useful discussion on writing ambitions and aspirations.

I allow about ten minutes for the initial information sharing and an additional ten if the mood of the group suggests they'd respond well to the publicity blurb route.

The only materials needed are copies of the handout and spare pens, pencils and paper for students who've forgotten their own.

In both situations, if the exercise reveals a large number of flower arrangers or Viking re-enactors, I set up an 'off-topic' forum online and suggest face-to-face students have a chat in the coffee-break.

The objective

This exercise helps to establish a group whose members recognise one another as individuals united by a shared interest in writing. Providing a pro forma may seem prescriptive but, especially when working online, I find it encourages shy students to get involved. It also provides boundaries for those who would otherwise tell their life story, usually to a level of detail I'd rather they didn't.

The exercise also offers possibilities for students to draw upon one another's expertise as an extension exercise later in the course, so adding a new dimension to writing what you know. This adds value to the basic exercise and reminds students that people they may initially perceive as too old/too young/too freaky/too boring invariably have something unexpected to share. It also encourages them to see their own experience as a valid and interesting resource – asking them to write a second version of their bio as a later exercise can help them go deeper into this idea.

From a lecturer's point of view, the basic exercise can help to identify the confident and chatty, the shy and also the difficult student and offer insights into the way they will interact as the course progresses.

With all groups, guidelines on giving and receiving feedback are part of the welcoming process, and may be summed up simply as 'treat others as you'd like to be treated'. This is especially important online when facelessness can embolden responses that would not be said face to face, so exercises that encourage the students to see one another as 'real people' have an important role.

Contributor: Elaine Walker
My full name is Judith Elaine. However, back in 1960 when I was born, 'a judy' was a slang name for a girl so my mother decided I'd be known as 'Elaine'. I write magical realist fiction, non-fiction and poetry – elaine-walker.com. I recommend *What if?: writing exercises for fiction writers* by Anne Bernays and Pamela Painter. Ask me if you need information on horses or the first Duke and Duchess of Newcastle. I can't help you with maths. If I didn't tell you, you never know that I'm lead singer in a rock band called Two Suns.

2

Writing animals

Introduction

Animals share our homes, our hearts, and our lives, and yet, writing about them is too often hampered by our inability to really know what it is to be animal. This experiential shortfall often causes new writers to rely on clichéd expressions and over-used phrases. Horses, for example are given human attributes, being described as 'brave' or 'noble' with coats like 'silk'; snakes are 'slimy', dogs 'bark', chickens 'squawk 'and pet rats 'stink', all of which fails to truly engage with animal subjects. The result is writing that is not only unoriginal but emotionally static and one dimensional.

I use the following exercises with my students to help overcome these limitations. They can be done in class or as homework and are best introduced at a point in the writing course when the students are comfortable enough to share their writing with the group.

The exercises rely strongly on memory and visualisation to invoke aspects of the animal through sensory recall. Students are asked to focus on the same animal throughout. Each section uses a similar pattern with students thinking about their animal by concentrating on each of the senses in turn, first through closed eyes using memory recall, and then by carrying out specific writing exercises.

The first four exercises should take between five and ten minutes each. When this phase has been completed, I give the students a further ten minutes to write a poem or word string to describe their animal, drawing on the material they have written.

The exercises
I begin by asking the students to close their eyes, then I give the following instructions, allowing time between each one for thinking and writing:

Touch
With your eyes closed, imagine what it feels like to touch your favourite animal. Touch it with different parts of your body such as your fingertips, your cheek, your nose, lips or bare legs. Think about the various sensations produced through contact with different parts of the animal.

Start with fur, feathers, scales, whiskers, teeth, claws, or hooves; then the muscles beneath the skin – the shape, length, and bulk; now the sinews, tendons and joints in limbs and tails.

Think next about the hard places – the bones and cartilage including the skull, ribs, ears, hips, knuckles and knees – and the soft places like the belly and paws.

Open your eyes and write about touch using a series of word strings encapsulated between descriptions of the human and animal points of contact e.g. 'cheek smooth satin soft curved tender cheek', 'lips fissured velvet prickles whiskers lips', 'finger tip leathery warm powdered quilled brushing tickles feathers bare skin cocky's comb finger tip'.

(continued overleaf)

Sound

Close your eyes again and think about the sounds your animal makes with its voice and its body; the long drawn-out howl, the sharp bark, toenails on linoleum, the thump a horse makes when it lies down, the silent gulp of a goldfish, the neighs, hisses, squawks and miaows. All these words name the sounds animals make but they don't describe them. Tune your ears and really listen to the difference in pitch, tone, volume and purpose for each vocalisation.

Open your eyes and make line drawings of these sounds. What words would you use to write the sounds you have drawn?

Smell

This time when you close your eyes, focus on the way your animal smells at certain times such as after a walk, or when it is wet, or in bed or after it has just eaten. Think about its breath, the smell of its coat, the soles of its feet.

Open your eyes and, using winemaker's language, make up phrases to describe the way your animal smells. e.g. 'damp with strong overtones of green horse manure infused with hints of powdery dust and summer grass'.

Taste

Close your eyes and now think about the times that you and your animal made oral contact. Perhaps you were tongue-kissed by your dog, or you smooched your horse on the nose, or accidentally inhaled a mouthful of cat spit. Maybe your favourite animal is the one you raise to eat. What do these experiences really taste like?

Open your eyes and make two parallel word lists you associate with the textures and flavours you experience when tasting your animal. Now make phrases from random word connections, e.g. 'dimpled halitosis', 'viscous rotting meat'.

Sight
Leave your eyes open and select those words and phrases from your lists that best describe your animal. Put the words together, either as a poem or a word string to create a brief visual picture of your animal.

Finally, I ask the students to read their descriptions aloud to the rest of the class and see how quickly someone can guess the kind of animal they are describing. A successful description will bring recognition, empathy and pleasure to the audience.

As homework follow-up, I ask them to take their notes and, if possible, to go and sit with the animal. Having spent some time beside it, they should consider how they have managed to capture it in language. Is their response authentic? Have they written the animal?

The objective
These exercises help creative writers to think outside the human, to fine tune their observational powers and discover fresh ways to write about animals. They represent a sensory approach that encourages students to describe their animal encounters through touch, sound, smell and taste, as well as the more usual starting point, sight. By adopting a phenomenological approach to writing that is more closely allied with the way animals operate in the world, students will experiment with ways to bring animals

into written language that are both original and authentic and ultimately, more appealing to potential readers.

Contributor: Sandra Burr
My full name is Sandra Elizabeth. I should have been called Elizabeth but it was my father's turn to name a child. I live in Canberra, Australia's capital city, surrounded by nature and the bush. I write creative non-fiction, non-fiction and poetry and am very fond of the personal essay. I recommend *The writing experiment: strategies for innovative creative writing* by Hazel Smith. Ask me if you want to know anything about why humans love horses. If I didn't tell you, you wouldn't know that I am enchanted by my Kindle.

3

Editing fiction: a process for creative critique

Introduction
This sustained collaborative exercise is drawn from my former role as a literary agent and editor. The activity it mirrors is sometimes called 'development editing': a process which eschews cosmetic polishing, seeking instead to ask powerful questions of a text, with the aim of prompting deep transformation.

I recommend introducing this towards the end of a course, so it reinforces and extends the skills students have already acquired. It's best undertaken over a few weeks: each stage requires a fresh eye, and confusion can set in if you try more than two in a sitting. Even so, exhaustive treatment is impossible – the trick is to maintain a brisk pace, and move on as soon as a viable line of enquiry emerges. Encouraging students to work independently between sessions ensures dynamic discussions and rich results.

The exercise
To begin, find a short story in the public domain that would benefit from editing. Cyberspace is full of them, but my preference is the newspaper Christmas story: the expediencies involved tend to result in highly entertaining but interestingly flawed fiction, with the added challenge of being by a well-known author. Reformat as a double-spaced manuscript, include appropriate acknowledgments,

and distribute before the first session. The only other resource you need is a flipchart.

STAGE 1: FIRST READING

Without preamble, invite students to air their immediate impressions. These may be pretty random, superficial and subjective – it doesn't matter. Write everything up without drawing conclusions or making links. Then detach those pages and put them aside. The point was simply to get all that off the collective chest, so the work can begin.

STAGE 2: CLOSE READING

Now arrange students in groups of three or four for collaborative work: the task is to reach an understanding of the text on its own terms. What kind of story is it? What is it really about? What are its patterns and structures? Which technical and stylistic features are generating meaning? I find it useful to roam around during group work, prompting students to develop their most interesting lines of enquiry.

Gather these observations, then ask for ideas about the potential of the story. Based on the close reading, how could this best be described? When a proposition emerges, formulate it as a sentence – for example: 'a darkly ironic love story, in which multiple points of view are choreographed to reveal the treachery and delusion of both protagonists'.

STAGE 3: TECHNICAL ANALYSIS

Forgetting the close reading for now, encourage the groups to scan all aspects of craft – tone, language, narrative position, characterisation, plot, pace, tense, thematic structure, form, use of dialogue, description, etc. – and to note whatever seems odd, inconsistent or unnecessary. The aim is to collect objective comments about the technical execution of the story, not to draw any firm conclusions.

Write these observations up and collect them under headings.

STAGE 4: POWERFUL QUESTIONS

Ask each group to compare the outcomes of the technical analysis with the outcomes of the close reading. Which specific technical issues seem to be preventing the story from achieving its potential? Gather all these ideas, write them up and then, in general discussion, start translating them into questions. For example: 'Why do the shifts in narrative perspective seem to take us away from the focus of the plot?'

Powerful questions are about the inner logic of the story, and are often about something that is missing. They might be philosophical, psychological, structural or linguistic – and it's likely that a number of equally fruitful lines of enquiry will emerge here. If you have the time, it's fascinating to pursue more than one, to see when – or if – they converge. But otherwise, use guided discussion to reach consensus on the most compelling question. For example: 'The tone and general effect are ironic – but what is the target of the irony?'

STAGE 5: POTENTIAL SOLUTIONS

Again using the outcomes of the close reading and technical analysis, encourage each group to imagine solutions. A good question will have multiple answers. For example, answers to the question above might be: 'character X – so his position in the narrative needs to shift'; 'the romance genre – this should be more apparent'; 'there's no target

– the tone is wrong'. Using these answers, ask groups to sketch out approaches to rewriting the story.

Collect these, and write them up.

STAGE 6: SENSE-CHECKING

Now encourage the groups to work through the suggested solutions, envisaging how they would play out in practice, and checking the implications on other narrative elements. Which solutions would cause more problems than they solve? Which seem to address the question best? Which seem too radical a departure from the story as it stands?

Use guided discussion to identify the most elegant solutions.

STAGE 7: COMMUNICATION

Finally, ask each group to draft an editorial letter to the author. This should begin with some comments based on the close reading, leading to a statement about the potential of the story. It should then identify the major technical issues, pose a question, and discuss a possible solution, whilst remaining open-ended, respectful and enthusiastic in tone. The purpose of the letter is to open a dialogue, not issue instructions.

Ask a member of each group to read their letter and encourage other students to adopt the position of author. How would they respond?

Conclude by drawing the best elements from the drafts to sketch out a final version of the letter.

The objective

The objective is to extend critical and self-reflexive skills towards vocational ends; empowering those students fortunate enough to find themselves in dialogue with an editor in the future, and also those who are inspired to use their abilities in the pursuit of salaried employment. In class, it's a confidence-building opportunity, using guided group discussion to follow a complex task through to a satisfying conclusion.

Contributor: Sam Kelly
My full name is Samantha Louise, though I don't believe my parents intended anything fancier than Sam. I write in the unaccountably neglected experimental art form of the essay. I recommend Raymond Queneau's *Exercises in style*. Ask me if you need information on the subcultures of miniaturists, or the joy of the Oulipo. I can't help you with directions, or anything involving the distinction between left and right. If I didn't tell you, you'd never know I play the flute – badly and enthusiastically – in a village ceilidh band.

4

On warming up, close reading and sentences

Introduction
As writers not only do we look to books for enjoyment but we often look to the texts we read, particularly those that excite and challenge us, to help us learn more about how to write and how to problem-solve issues as we edit and rewrite our own work. In this context we are influenced and taught by the books we read. I teach a class in which the close reading of texts works in tandem with short risk-taking writing exercises, both in class and as 'homework' between classes. This sort of hybrid classroom situation is where these exercises will work best.

The exercises
All students need for the warm-up exercises is something to write on/with. In these exercises, close reading discussions alternate with writing practices. These exercises can be done in the same week, or in consecutive weeks, with texts of your choosing. The texts you choose should have particularly well-constructed or controversial sentences and paragraphs. My favourite texts for these exercises are Gertrude Stein's *Three lives*, Ernest Hemingway's *The old man and the sea*, and the last breath poems of Katie Ford in her book *Deposition*.

If you can, it's best to assign the reading before class or find a strong piece that is easy to read and discuss as a handout/projection. Reading out each piece can help students find a way into discussing sentences as distinct entities and then as building blocks for paragraphs, characters and stories. This also introduces reading aloud as a crucial practice in a writer's self-editing.

Warm-up exercises
WORDS INTO SENTENCES

As a class, have students choose and write down five words. The words should not relate to each other either in sound or meaning. Encourage an acrobatic, elastic and non-sensical word play in this free writing exercise where they include all five words. Have them loosen the ties to logic or meaning and allow the words to sound together, roll into each other, away from each other. Allow five minutes and then time for a quick sharing.

Have them choose a sentence they particularly like and write it out on a new line. Use the *last* word of this sentence as the *first* word of the next and repeat. To up the stakes, you can ask students to tell a story while maintaining the first/last principle.

BEST/WORST

Have students circle the best sentence from the pieces they've written, and underline one that needs work. They then read out their sentences and talk about what works or doesn't work and why. I use this opportunity to draw attention to elements of sentence construction that will be useful for all students to be aware of. For example, I explain that a sentence can be strong and weak – – as in the idea is strong, but not yet realised in the language, or it has fantastic phrasing but doesn't belong anywhere beyond this practice. Through the resulting discussion, students can start to distinguish between both strong and weaker

17

writing and move beyond like/dislike. This grounds them in the how and why of critical reading that will prove useful when discussing someone like Stein.

Close reading and exercises on sentences and paragraphs

CLOSE READ: SENTENCES

Choose a text, focusing on the sentences. I like to use Stein's *Three lives* because her sentences build character and story in a way that is useful for analysis. We read a few extracts, discussing the sentences and how they function in the stories. I draw attention to the way her varied repetition is closely held within paragraphs as well as being a structural tool throughout the piece to concretely express thought and behaviour patterns. I also focus on how she layers adjectives in an asynchronous way to build unique characters, situations and stories.

WRITING EXERCISE: SENTENCES

Choose a paragraph from Stein and a random, simple subject, like buying an apple, and have students write a scene for ten minutes, aiming to be Stein-esque. They can be reverent or irreverent, as long as they can talk about the elements of craft they played with. I always explain at this point that we don't have to like an author to learn from them. Have them share their creations, discussing not only their sentences and repetition, but how using linguistic triggers affected their writing and identifying strengths and weaknesses in what they have written.

CLOSE READ: PARAGRAPHS

Hemingway builds his sentences in less noticeable way. From *The old man and the sea* read the section in the first few pages where the boy and the old man go to the old man's shack. Ask how the language is working and draw attention to the way Hemingway includes a detail or object in a sentence, then carries it to the next sentence – usually with a noticeably different context/structure – then lets it drop as he picks up another item or detail. The paragraph builds in complexity as each detail, each sentence, builds into a solid, satisfying description and moves into character and emotional resonance too.

WRITING EXERCISE: PARAGRAPHS

This exercise loosens the reins again, and gives the students the opportunity to consider how their reading has influenced how they think about sentences and repetition and details and then apply those ideas to their own writing. With these things in mind, have them write a scene of action/place like climbing a tree, making a cup of tea, or entering the room of someone who is dying.

The objective

These exercises, including their format in which close reading leads to a writing practice, are set up to directly link our close reading of texts to our own writing. They focus on the practical application of looking at the construction of sentences and paragraphs, but you could also use similar exercises and focus on elements like influence and homage as well.

Contributor: Elizabeth Reeder

My name is Elizabeth K. Reeder. I write fiction: long, short and for radio as well as crossover pieces that could be called lyrical essays or poems. Subjects I'm writing about now

19

are: fire, architecture, memory and prairies – visit ekreeder.
com. *Reading like a writer* by Francine Prose is the book I
recommend. Ask me about exuberance, death and radical
essaying. If I didn't tell you, you wouldn't know that I
used to be a contemporary dancer.

5

Travel writing – from classroom to Khartoum

Introduction
The difficulty in asking students to produce a piece of travel writing for an in-class exercise is that they are stuck in a seminar room, unable to travel anywhere – except, of course, in their memories. So this is where a practical session can initiate the process of transforming personal experience into narrative. No matter whether the memory is of a wet weekend in Bournemouth or a trek through the rainforest of Borneo, travel is a rich, often untapped and unappreciated, resource for a student writer.

This two-hour class, based closely on one I designed for a life writing module I'm teaching on an English and writing BA programme, introduces students to travel writing as a sub-genre of autobiography but one that often traverses other narrative categories.

The exercise – setting up
Some students may not see how their family holiday, exchange visit or backpacking trip could possibly be of interest to anyone but themselves. Travel as a source of amusing anecdotes to be shared with friends on Facebook is one thing, but travel *writing*? So, time spent at the beginning of the session in establishing a practical and theoretical context is useful not just in breaking down resistance to the notion but, importantly, in giving students a sense of how their experiences as travellers might be harnessed creatively.

I open by asking the students to jot down a few notes about a journey, trip or holiday that sticks in their memory. I make the point that it doesn't need to have been a dramatic adventure in a spectacularly exotic location. After a few minutes, I invite a couple of students to read out their notes, prompting them to elaborate along the way.

I often find they need to be encouraged to give an impression of the setting as well as the events that occurred there and to reflect, not merely recount. Shaped by the right questions, the selected students will, in summary at least, produce oral stories of their particular travel experiences that illustrate to the whole group how a few bullet-point notes can be worked up into the makings of a narrative that integrates the place with the personal.

At this point I distribute an extract from Haslam and Neale, *Life writing* (pp.117–120), in which Derek Neale interviews Jenny Diski about the synthesis of autobiography and travel narrative in her work. After allowing the group time to read the excerpt, I open out a discussion about the issues it raises and how these might apply to their own travel writing. From here, I pose a set of questions for the students to consider in relation to the pieces they are about to write. To what extent is the physical geography of the place they visited integral to their account? What of the human geography – the people they met, the cultural or social differences they encountered? What do they know of the place's history and current political situation and how might this be relevant? Was this trip personally significant to them in some way? In essence, I am inviting the students to describe, reflect and contextualise, not just chronicle a sequence of events.

The exercise – writing

At this point, usually mid-way through the session, or a little beyond if the discussion elements have gone well, the students are ready to write. I ask them to refer to the notes they made at the outset, using them as the starting point for an extended piece of writing about that particular travel experience. I offer them a choice between using:
a) the present tense, as though it is happening now; or
b) the past tense, reflecting on the trip with hindsight.

I explain that what they will produce in class is a work-in-progress to be developed further in their own time. The imposition of a word limit will depend on my aims for them at the time and the nature of the course. What's more important is to stress the need to control their subject matter; a common pitfall with this exercise is that some students try to write about an entire holiday or backpacking trip where a narrower focus on one episode or aspect would be more effective. I usually allow forty-five minutes' writing time.

At wrap-up, I point out that developing the pieces they've just begun will require them to draw on research material to check facts and to consolidate the narrative. I outline the range of sources open to them, including their own records, such as travel journals and photographs, as well as maps, guide books and online information about the place they visited.

The objective

This session aims to get students started on a piece which will be much more substantial and interesting than a 'What I did in the holidays' essay of the type we all recall so fondly (or not) from our school days. It invites them to consider questions of subjectivity and objectivity when turning autobiographical experience into a reflective narrative – one rooted in fact but steeped in the writer's personal impressions of a journey or place.

They also learn how to be selective in deciding which elements of their trip to include and which to leave out. They discover that travel writing, although a branch of non-fiction, nonetheless requires skills more usually associated with fiction – presentation of character, scene setting and evocation of place, development of a narrative thread or 'story', and the narration of dramatic set-pieces. Like a novelist, the travel writer creates a world in the reader's imagination.

Above all, the exercise helps students to appreciate that the best travel writers take an inner journey as well as an outer one, that there are two subjects: the travel and the traveller.

Contributor: Martyn Bedford

My middle name is Corby, my grandmother's maiden name – oh, how my school friends laughed. I write fiction for adults and teenagers – see http://www.martynbedford.com – and teach at Leeds Trinity University College in the north of England. I recommend *The writer's workbook* edited by Jenny Newman, Edmund Cusick and Aileen La Tourette. When I'm not writing, I feel uneasy. Ask me about the physical and metaphysical geography of Ilkley Moor but don't expect any help with DIY. If I didn't tell you, you would never know that, between the ages of thirteen and nineteen, I refereed more than 200 football matches.

6

The flexibility of free indirect style

Introduction

When I began writing fiction in earnest, responding readers in university writing workshops would sometimes make comments in this vein: 'This word here – *limn* – doesn't seem like a word this character would use. *Limn* doesn't sound like Mrs Finkel, as I know her from this story.' My initial reaction was that, well, of course Mrs Finkel wouldn't use limn. What an erroneous reading, what a ridiculous thing to say! Mrs Finkel's not talking! *Limn* was, in my mind, the narrator's word – and the narrator's the only one, by definition, telling the story.

My readers, I now know, understood and were applying a concept, perhaps too stringently, that I neither understood nor deliberately applied. They were assuming free indirect style in my story. They believed that, since Mrs Finkel seemed to be the protagonist, the narrative was somehow filtered through her consciousness. They were reading for the narrative language to *reflect* my character's language and thinking.

To help my students grasp this concept earlier in their development than I did, I give a 'starter definition' of free indirect style as a blending of an outside, third-person narrative voice with the voice of a character's consciousness. I find it helps to ask them to think first about their own manifold voices: the one they use to deliver public speeches, the one they use to talk intimately with friends, the private one they use when facing down their best and worst thoughts.

They need to understand that in a story where free indirect style is employed, readers receive narration at times through the filter of an outside narrator and at times through the filter of a character's mind. I explain that this is the move writers often refer to as 'going inside the head' of a character and that 'indirect' refers to the lack of a signal phrase attributing thought.

A simple handout showing how it works can be useful for them to refer to as they complete the exercise:

DIRECTLY ATTRIBUTED THOUGHT: He moved from room to room, cursing at himself. Nobody knew what he was going through, he thought to himself.

FREE INDIRECT STYLE: He moved from room to room, cursing at himself. Nobody in this whole goddamned world knew what he was going through.

In the above instance of free indirect style, the word *goddamned* indicates that the narrator has 'gone inside the head' of the 'he' character. 'He' uses the word *goddamned*, but perhaps the narrator would not.

The narrator has temporarily suspended her direct filtration of events. She's gone *indirect*. We are getting narrative – in this case, a reporting of the character's thoughts – filtered primarily through the consciousness of the character.

The exercise

Ask students to write a bit of expository prose – perhaps a description of the baggage-claim area of a busy airport at midday – from the point-of-view of this character:

An author of fine works of literature, a keen observer, who has masterful and precise diction, neither too stuffy nor too casual. This author is observing a visibly distraught young person, a stranger, waiting for his/her bags to arrive. About why the stranger is distraught, the keen observer has no direct knowledge.

Writing time: 5–10 minutes

Next, using the same setting (baggage-claim area of busy airport, midday), write a bit of expository prose from the point-of-view of this character:

A young person, perhaps a student, dressed casually but not provocatively, who has just returned home after a long absence. He/she waits at the baggage claim. Something significant in this character's external life has recently changed. Thoughts of this change seem to *intrude* on his/her thinking.

Writing time: 5–10 minutes

When students are finished with the second character's exposition, ask them to pause a moment. Have them read both pieces aloud, perhaps in pairs or trios. Then, talk as a group about what they heard. What choices did the writers make to differentiate the two voices? What do those choices – about diction, syntax, speed of delivery, sentence length, willingness or unwillingness to think or to express certain thoughts – tell us about each character, who they are and what they're all about?

Now, ask students to attempt yet another bit of expository prose, a third piece of writing taking another ten to fifteen minutes, that blends these first two voices together in this way: the narrative begins in the voice of the distanced, observant 'authorial' narrator, but then eventually *slips* into the voice – i.e. uses the diction, the syntax, the manner of speaking and thinking – of the young person whose life has recently changed. At this point, the two voices should now seem established and distinct in the writers' minds. Toward the end of the writing time, at about the ten-minute mark, instruct the students to attempt to *slip* back into the voice of the distanced observer.

The exercise can be completed with a read-round and discussion.

The objective

What do we gain from free indirect style? Narrative flexibility, I think: the conjoined possibilities of distant, observant or character-revealing narration. In this short exercise, students will have built themselves access to the keen observer, the narrator who can see the baggage claim and the distraught young person from the outside, and the distressed young person whose internal life has been shaken by a dramatic external change. By establishing both voices independently at first, students can then perhaps find a way to move between them. If a student decides to continue with this story, she'll now have available both polar voicings as well as myriad possibilities along the spectrum between. She'll have achieved, at least once, a free indirect style.

Contributor: Richard B. Sonnenmoser

My middle name is Barthelme, and, surely because of that, I've always been magnetically pulled to the fiction of Donald Barthelme. I live in Maryville, Missouri, where I teach creative writing at Northwest Missouri State University and co-edit *The Laurel Review*. I write fiction and poetry. My chapbook, *Science-magic school*, won the 2010 Midnight Sun Poetry Chapbook Contest. I recommend Charles Baxter's *The art of subtext*. Ask me if you need information on cropping tobacco. I can't help you with your haircut. You'd never have known if I hadn't told you that as a child I confused lucid dreams with memories.

7

The blue chip exercise: defying a single aspect of 'reality' in short fiction

Introduction
I use this exercise early in a fiction writing class. It provides focused writing practice on a fictional narrative by allowing the student to overturn a single scientific principle within a story opening. It can be used to engage students who may be frustrated by restrictions they've encountered in other classes that discourage genre fiction or that disallow anything but literary realism.

The inspiration for this exercise is from a tangentially-related revision prompt in Stone and Nyren, *Deepening fiction*, which brought to light for me the prevalence of reality-defying stories in classical and contemporary work. I've reverse-engineered it based on such literary models. This can be a playful assignment that rewards creativity at any level of fiction writing. Some students turn this opening into their longer, main story for the course.

The exercise
I give my students the following handout – the blue chip mentioned isn't, of course, real. It's merely a metaphor, an imaginary coin that purchases a single breach of 'reality'.

The blue chip
Write the first five pages of a short story. You have one blue chip to spend in this opening. The blue chip allows you to defy a single aspect of 'reality'. Spend your blue chip to break a single law of physics or accepted scientific principle. For example, in Franz Kafka's story, 'Metamorphosis' (*Metamorphosis and other stories*), a man wakes up one morning having been transformed into an insect – not something that science would endorse as a possibility. Note that Gregor Samsa doesn't also levitate or shoot fire from his mouth: the conceit and the story would become absurd if those occurred. Beyond the initial violated principle, your story should adhere to realism. Spend your blue chip somewhere in the first five pages.

The model
It works well to read and discuss a published model before assigning this exercise. Instead of 'The Metamorphosis', which is longish for a short story, I've used Steven Millhauser's story, 'Flying carpets', (*The knife thrower and other stories*), which is about just that; and Greg Hrbek's 'Sagittarius' (*The best American short stories 2009*), which includes as one of its characters a centaur child born to a married couple. For a model, any story that breaks a single aspect of 'reality' will do.

Modifying the exercise
Requiring only an opening can have mixed results. On the one hand, it's a fast exercise that students can produce in a week or less. On the other hand, some students find the restriction of writing only an opening frustrating since

31

their narrative inevitably is incomplete. It also can make critiquing more difficult since it's harder to comment on an opening's effectiveness without knowing where the story's headed. Thus, if you have time, it's preferable to require a full story.

I find that some students like to use this exercise to give their characters a superhuman power. One of the stronger stories I've seen from it was about a teenage boy who discovers a special flexibility in his neck that he develops until he can turn his head around 360 degrees; he earns and then loses the admiration of his peers as a result of his special skill.

That example notwithstanding, in order to avoid an excess of werewolves, vampires and characters who can incinerate others with their eyes – to push students, in other words, toward the emotional realism at the heart of this exercise – it can be helpful to add a note that the violated principle doesn't need to be a special power. In many literary examples, in fact, the supernatural phenomenon is something visited upon the characters in a way that often upsets their lives and illuminates, somehow, the human condition.

The objective

By addressing the fantasy/realism divide, this exercise helps the class begin to talk about the importance of believable characters. Even if a story includes something improbable – and perhaps *especially* then – it must have compelling characters. The heightened situations that result when a physical law is broken are not easy to write convincingly. I find that, paradoxically, by allowing students to include a fantastical element in a story opening, they're encouraged to focus on realistic character reactions and authenticating details.

Similarly, this exercise engages the tension between genre and literary fiction in that one criticism typically leveled at genre stories, especially fantasy and science fiction, is that they spend too much time developing their worlds. Introducing a single fantastical element can make for many distractions within a short story, a test of the writer's ability to strike the right balance between world, character, and plot.

While students ought to be encouraged to give free rein to their imaginations in the drafting phase of this exercise, ideally in revision they will be alert for metaphorical possibilities that arise, cultural critiques, deeper connections that broaden the story's meaning.

Contributor: Jeff P. Jones
I was named with the hope that my initials, J.P. Jones, redolent of wealthy industrialists, might one day come in handy when I took the helm of a major international bank; needless to say, my parents have been sorely disappointed. I live in northern Idaho and write fiction and non-fiction. I recommend that you read Priscilla Long's *The writer's portable mentor*. Ask me if you'd like to have your new blend of coffee taste-tested. I can't help you with chemistry or appliance repair.

8

Teaching aspects of minimalism:
flash and micro fiction

Introduction

Short stories can be tricky things to teach. Henderson and Hancock describe how short fiction has often been the most subversive form, defying traditional novelistic traits, remaining deliberately elusive and resistant to easy interpretation (*Short fiction and critical contexts*, pp. xix–xx). Getting the balance between what is explicitly told and what remains 'off the page' can frustrate professional writers, let alone students unfamiliar with the form. What I'd like to do is suggest two exercises that can be used to help students explore these ideas in their writing. By doing so, the students will be exploring aspects of minimalism.

Each exercise uses a modern variant of the short story: flash and micro fiction. By flash fiction I mean the writing of discrete stories that are less than one thousand words in length; micro fiction is taken to be even shorter, a story of thirty words or less. Both have seen enormous growth in popularity, driven in part by the proliferation of web-based flash fiction sites. Few competitions now do not have a flash fiction category, and publishers are waking up to the potential of short stories delivered and read through mobile applications.

Short stories also have an exciting role to play in our workshops, certainly as a way of introducing these new narrative forms to students, but also as a means by which students can learn techniques that apply to all forms of fiction writing.

Micro fiction

OVERVIEW

This exercise encourages the student to consider one important parameter of creative writing, namely *word length*, exploring how few words are actually needed to tell a complete and effective story.

A limit of thirty words for this exercise still provides opportunity for a degree of complexity in the narrative while being rigorous enough to make the student think very carefully about the story and what actually needs to be written down.

The exercise

The full exercise can be done within one hour, assuming a class of twenty students. This is a good exercise for first-year undergraduates but can be used more generally as an introductory session on any course and is very effective as an ice-breaker.

The exercise timings are as follows:

0–30 MINUTES

Students are introduced to the concept of micro fiction and then write their own micro fiction on a piece of paper.

30–60 MINUTES

Each student passes their micro fiction round the group. These are read by all students. Finally, the group is asked to decide on their favourite three, and more importantly, to explain their choice.

The objective

The exercise facilitates a discussion about *narrative technique*, especially in regard to short story writing. The best micro fiction tends to work rather like good haiku, remaining abstract and elusive, suggestive of a plot rather than trying to directly represent it on the page. This idea of abstraction has links with minimalism more generally, a key technique within short story writing. The thirty-word story tempts students out of their comfort zone, empowering them to think abstractly.

Flash fiction and the 'four layer model'

OVERVIEW

The 'four layer model' provides students with a useful template when writing flash fiction. Specifically, it offers a tool by which they can experiment with one key idea of the shorter form of fiction writing – that of *abstraction*, of keeping much of the story off the page. This has associations with another key technique in creative writing, of course – *showing*, not *telling*. However, the 'four layer model' supports the examination of a more extreme approach, the *iceberg effect*, in which much of the story remains unsaid, but is instead implied or inferred through action and dialogue. For flash fiction, this remains an extremely important technique.

WHAT IS THE 'FOUR LAYER MODEL'?

The 'four layer model' is an abstract representation of a short story. Think of it as layers of cake, one on top of the other. The bottom layer represents the *theme* of the story; the layer on top of that represents *character backgrounds and relationships*. We then have *story events to this point*, events that are outside of the story, but which still impinge upon it; and then finally *scene(s) in the story*, in other words what is actually written on the page.

The exercise
The full exercise can be done within a two-hour workshop, assuming a class of twenty students, and is especially useful for first-year undergraduates.

The exercise timings are as follows:
0–20 MINUTES
Introduction to the 'four layer model'.
20–60 MINUTES
Each student proposes a short scene involving two characters. The student then outlines details for each of the three 'hidden' layers of the 'four layer model': *story events to this point, character background and relationships,* and *theme(s).*
60–90 MINUTES
Each student then begins writing a full story of no more than a thousand words, drawing on these three layers of the model.
90–120 MINUTES
The students pass their work around. The group is asked to discuss the degree to which such an approach to writing either helps or hinders the narrative.

The objective
The exercise facilitates a discussion about the writing process and the degree to which good flash fiction requires planning and careful preparation. It also introduces the student to the idea of withholding key detail. In this sense, the 'four layer model' is a good template by which

students can experiment with ideas of minimalism in their writing.

Contributor: Spencer Jordan
My parents tell me that the inspiration for my first name was Winston Spencer Churchill and not, definitely not, Spencer Tracy. I write historical fiction – see http://www3.uwic. ac.uk/English/education/staffprofiles/Pages/ Spencer J Bio.aspx. I recommend *Writing fiction: a guide to narrative craft* by Janet Burroway and Elizabeth Stuckey-French. When I'm not writing, I like to get out into the Welsh hills and mountains. Ask me about nineteenth century Bristol; do not ask me about Lady Gaga. If I didn't tell you, you'd never know that I'm related to Charles II.

9

Out of solitude: collaborative fiction writing

Introduction
I often find that students remain silent in early class sessions, and their first stories similarly feature characters sitting alone in rooms rather than engaging with other characters. Sometimes students lack the confidence to create multiple characters or their own shyness bleeds into their fiction. This exercise is designed to overcome both physical and fictional silences, as students must communicate so their characters can share scenes together. It can work well for a first fiction class.

This exercise is derived from an experiment I tried with my own writing as an undergraduate with my colleague Heather Wilson. It was further influenced by Raymond Queneau's *Exercises in style*. I adapted my original experiment for use in my classroom. The exercise is easiest when there is an even number of students to place into pairs, but I have had groups of three successfully complete it as well.

The exercise
Place the students into pairs or groups of three, ideally not with anyone they already know, as part of the exercise is to get them talking to new people.

Each student is asked to come up with a very basic outline of a character, and these characters will interact through the remainder of the exercise. The characters can be friends, enemies, strangers, family – any type of relationship is possible. The characters also do not have to be human. A group once wrote about a cow and a pig meeting over the counter at a butcher shop, where the twist was that the meat for sale was human, not animal.

Students outline a scenario in which their characters are together in one location (work, social setting, outdoors, indoors, etc.). They then devise an opening scene where the characters interact and speak. It is important that each student writes their own copy of the scene, for two reasons. First, they will need to have a complete copy to finish at home, and second, while the dialogue should be identical in both versions of the story, the students should begin working with point of view. What type of things do their characters notice? How does each character feel about what is happening?

The next stage of the writing exercise involves the characters separating for a length of chronological time. Here the stories will vary – each student will trace what happens to their character over the time they are apart. Do they meet other people? Carry out a task? Go to work, school or the park? Anything is possible.

In the third stage of the exercise, the characters meet again and have another dialogue exchange. The events in the middle of the story will impact upon their final conversations.

The second and third stages of the exercise are usually completed outside of the classroom. Students often exchange email addresses, but I encourage them to meet in person on campus or to use a virtual learning environment (if possible) to communicate if they do not wish to share personal contact details. The following week, the stories are read and workshopped in class. It is a strong hook for an opening workshop, as the differences between the stories give students a clear opportunity to discuss and analyse the possibilities of storytelling.

Practical considerations
Allow twenty to thirty minutes for the first stage of the exercise in class. The only materials needed are paper and pens or pencils.

As with any collaborative writing exercise at any level, it is vital that one participant does not end up dictating the direction of the group. The lecturer needs to offer support by going around the room to chat to each group individually during the first stage. As this is usually the first group exercise I run in a workshop, I find that students sometimes need assistance both to bridge the conversational gaps and to convince them it is safe to share their ideas. I can be a conduit for ideas from the quieter students – who will often speak to a lecturer but not a fellow student – so the ideas of the whole group can be heard and utilised.

For students who claim to have no ideas at all, I try to highlight similarities between group members. For example, I had three male students who struggled with the exercise until I pointed out they were the only students in the class with facial hair – they raced off to begin a story about beards. Since this exercise comes early in my workshops, I try to keep the atmosphere as light and enjoyable as possible and to encourage students to stretch their imaginations as far as they will go.

The objective
The exercise encourages students away from introspective openings where characters do nothing except sit in a dark

41

room and think and also establishes working relationships early in the class. Students have to start talking and inventing promptly, as they do not have long to complete the first stage of the exercise in class. This is a deliberate strategy, as working together to a deadline helps to cement a relationship. For the lecturer, moving around the groups and listening to their ideas gives a strong insight into the students' confidence, creativity and their willingness to share within a group.

The results of this exercise can work well for a first workshopping session. Not only do the differences between the characters' experience give wide openings for discusssion, but students often have increased confidence due to the fact that at least one other student has read their writing before sharing it with the entire group.

Contributor: Jennifer Young
My full name is Jennifer Maria. Jennifer came from a diaper commercial, and Maria springs from *The sound of music*, although my mother convinced my father it was a variation on his middle name, Marion. My Southern Gothic writing is set in my native North Carolina and my dystopian fiction is set in London, my adopted home. Most weekends find me baking and playing Scrabble. I recommend *The 3 a.m. epiphany: uncommon writing exercises that transform your fiction* by Brian Kiteley. If I didn't tell you, you'd never know I'm a member of the landlocked Kentish Town Yacht Club.

10

Being (in)famous: getting into character

Introduction

I am based in the Netherlands, where the first milestone creative writing course in higher education did not begin until 2011. Therefore, like all creative writing tutors in Holland, I have a background in teaching through the amateur arts sector. Students, usually known as 'course members', are people of all ages with varied educational backgrounds. They may plan to take just a single course or to develop a more serious long-term interest. Therefore, the classes have to be pleasurable and accessible for people taking writing lessons primarily for their enjoyment as well as those who may plan to go on to further study. Without losing sight of the value of or desired response to the exercise, my exercises are developed with that 'fun factor' in mind.

The exercise

In this exercise, which I like to call 'image writing', the students are asked to think of someone famous with a well-known reputation. In a plenary setting, we make a list of these people who are either very popular or notorious. Names currently in the news for being spoiled and tiresome, or arrogant and hard to handle, tend to come up. This means that most participants know who the people on the list are and may have an opinion on their behaviour already.

I then ask each student to choose one famous person from the list and to write a monologue written in that person's voice. In this monologue – which can be, for example, a letter to fans or a post on a website – the famous person has to reveal a dark secret that does not match their usual public profile or reputation. After a writing time, usually around ten minutes, the monologues are read out loud. This usually leads to a light-hearted discussion on perceptions, assumptions and public personas. With more confident groups, I would lead this into a discussion on credibility of voice and the way in which each monologue both engages with and challenges accepted perceptions of the famous person it supposedly presents.

The objective
This is a good exercise to start a course with as students, especially the young ones, tend to be a bit tense and insecure during a first class. A 'lightweight' exercise like this loosens up the writing muscles as well as the general mood. I developed this exercise during a course on character building. It helps students understand that a character is a person with an individual register of traits and that once created, these start to shape the writing.

The exercise also encourages students who are still a bit hesitant to write creatively as it's relatively easy to write as if you were a person with an almost caricature personality. While encouraging students to get involved it provides boundaries for those who tend to let their characters run wild and make them incredible by showing them it's easy to let your character speak or act 'out of character'. From a lecturer's point of view, this exercise can help to identify students who can already write outside the box, by revealing a character's unexpected and bold secret, and those who will need extra help letting their inner creative writer emerge.

Contributor: Diana Chin-A-Fat
My Chinese surname is a contraction from my great-great-grandfather's surname (Chin) and my great-grandfather's first name (A-Fat). At least, I think that's the story. I live in a dike house, in a small village near Rotterdam in the Netherlands. I primarily write book reviews for a Dutch national newspaper. When I'm not writing, I like to take long walks with my dog while I think of last minute rewrites of my latest book review. Ask me if you need information on creative writing in the Netherlands. If I didn't tell you, you'd never know that I always secretly wanted to be a prima ballerina.

11

Make your own manifesto:
a playful approach to purposeful writing

Introduction
This is a mildly competitive exercise, in which students attempt to recruit new members to their invented literary movements through the medium of the manifesto. It's ideal for large classes and is best developed over a few consecutive weeks. I teach in three-hour sessions, and generally run this exercise over four half-sessions. One caveat: it's better not to try it near the beginning of a course, as students will need time to get to know each other first. And an advert: this is probably the most fun I've ever had in a classroom.

The exercise
WEEK 1 – PREPARATION
What you will need:
Examples of manifestos
Plenty of breakout space for group work
Flipcharts and pens
A handout for your students with the following questions:

> How would you characterise the dominant culture right now?
>
> What do you think is phony?
>
> What is over-rated?
>
> What assumptions should be challenged?
>
> What makes you angry?
>
> What do you believe in?
>
> What can you do that's new?

Start the first session with a brief talk on the manifesto as an art form and the literary movement as an agent for change, with a gallop through the most obvious avant-gardes of Modernism. All I try to do here is sketch the kinds of political and aesthetic assumptions that each movement set out to disrupt, give a sense of the inspired and ludicrous wrangling within and between successive movements, and demonstrate some of the radical shifts in writing that occurred as a result.

After this, explain that the task in broad terms is to form movements and invent manifestos to be performed to a voting audience in three weeks' time, then give the students a few minutes to get themselves into groups. There's no need for groups to be even, and I find it best not to be prescriptive: depending on the size of the class, groups of anything from two to six work well.

Ask the groups to disperse into breakout areas and give each one a selection of manifestos to look at. The Futurist, Imagist, Vorticist, DADA, Surrealist and Situationist manifestos are all available online – some, happily, in their original typography – and it's worth mixing in some contemporary examples. Among my favourites is China Miéville's *Rejectamentalist.* During this time, it's useful to roam around the groups, answering questions, offering observations and guiding discussions.

Finally, distribute the handout of questions to each group and ask them to note their thoughts. During this, and all the subsequent group work, it's better if you don't roam around – it's much more fun if the students are working in secret.

WEEK 2 – GROUP WORK
The groups work in the breakout areas with flipcharts, pens and examples of manifestos, to continue their discussions. Situate yourself in your own space, ready to give advice or answer questions – and at intervals during the session, distribute the following two handouts.

WHAT YOUR MOVEMENT IS FOR
How would you define it, intellectually?
How would you demonstrate it, artistically?
How would you persuade others of it?

EACH MOVEMENT SHOULD HAVE:
a name;
a political or philosophical standpoint;
an aesthetic proposition;
an enemy;
some rules of engagement (e.g. membership criteria, a dress code, actions which must be performed by members, mandatory writing techniques).
Note: all of these should be included in your manifesto.

Week 3 – group work

Exactly as Week 2, with this final handout distributed once discussions are underway.

Grand presentations

This is a competition: there will be an invited audience, and your aim is to recruit the largest number of new members to your movement.

You will have twenty minutes to present your manifesto.

You may use handouts, audiovisual material, and any additional tactics you choose.

The audience may ask you questions before voting.

Week 4 – presentations

You will need:

- invited audience members (colleagues, former students, guest lecturers, etc.);
- plenty of cakes and sweets;
- a hat and lots of slips of paper.

To begin, get each movement to write their name on a slip of paper, and draw them from the hat to determine the order of presentations. Distribute cakes and sweets; sit back and enjoy hearing them. After each presentation, allow a few minutes for audience questions.

Voting is by secret ballot – use the slips of paper and hat. Students must vote on the movement they would join if their own didn't exist; invited audience members vote for whichever movement they found most amusing or persuasive. Count votes, announce results, applaud the winner, and finish up all the cake.

The objective

I devised this exercise with only one aim in mind: to introduce more entertaining collaborative work to my sessions. The manifestos my classes create range from the deeply heartfelt, through pointed satire, to the downright bonkers. The presentations are always excellent creative mayhem, with some amazing writing, a lot of dressing up and declaiming, and much vigorous argument. Past students have gone on to design and publish pamphlets, and been invited to stage their manifestos at new writing events.

Student feedback on this experience is always effusive, and I've found it to be a real turning point in the group dynamic; increasing confidence, openness and willingness to debate. Later in the course, I've used the manifestos as a way of opening up other topics, by inviting the class to get back into character to discuss a particular issue.

The most pleasing side effect I've observed is a change in the students' approach to self-reflection. Following this exercise, self-reflexive essays have become more active and purposeful, with students showing an increased desire to consider not only what their own work is, but also what it might be *for*.

Contributor: Sam Kelly

My full name is Samantha Louise. My mum was inspired by *Bewitched*, though Dad, convinced I would be a boy, continued to call me Gavin for some time. I write rarely: my vocation is to empower the creative thinking and practice of others. I recommend James Wood's *How fiction works*. Ask me if you need information on what literary agents really do, or how Derrida can change your life. I can't help you with getting things off high shelves. If I didn't tell you, you'd never know I can skin and gut a brace of pheasant in twenty minutes flat.

12

Yoga on the page: moving into writing

Introduction

I find that yoga and writing work well together because of basic similarities. Both stretch us, increase flexibility and encourage us to go deeper inside ourselves. It is easy to forget that writing is physical. I like to think of the writing process as starting in the heart, moving up to the brain, down the arm, and into the hand. And yoga is not just about twisting the body into a pretzel. It is about breathing, openness and meditation. So, both yoga and writing are a synthesis of body, mind and spirit.

The following exercises are designed to be done in a chair and can easily be done in a classroom. They aim to relax the mind, loosen the body, ease the student into creative writing and leave them with techniques they can practise on their own.

Opening yoga exercises

Begin the class by asking the group to place their hands on their chests, close their eyes and chant the mantra Om three times, explaining that this is known as the sound of the universe and as the universal word. This allows each person to feel a vibration run through them and also brings the group together in sound.

Then ask them to do the following, keeping the instructions slow and allowing time for each stage:

1. Rub the hands together to create heat and place the

head in the hands, feeling the weight we carry around all day.

2. Move the head up and down in a 'yes' movement three times, then shake it in a 'no' movement three times.
3. Rotate the head all the way around to the right three times, then to the left three times.
4. Massage the neck to work out any knots and rotate the wrists, three times to the left, then right.
5. While still seated, clasp the hands together behind the back. Breathe in and bend forward towards the knees, then breathe out and straighten up – continue breathing and bending up and down eight times.
6. Sitting up straight, place the left hand on the right knee and the right hand on the small of the back. Breathing in, turn the torso to the right. Turn the head over the right shoulder. Take a few breaths in and out. Do the same going the opposite way.
7. Scrunch up the face, bring the shoulders up to the ears, and make tight fists. Take a deep breath in and when breathing out roar like a lion. Do this three times.

Opening writing exercise

The lion exercise usually results in some laughter, adding to the relaxed feeling inspired by the stretches, so this is a good time to start writing. Inspired by Kathleen Adams' 'five minute sprint' in *The way of the journal: a journal therapy workbook for healing*, pp. 18–20, I've adapted this exercise to allow students to bring a bodily experience into their writing. I encourage quick writing without stopping in order to avoid the internal censor.

Ask the students to close their eyes and to take three deep breaths in and out, suggesting that they begin to feel comfortable in this space and in themselves. Use the prompt *How do you feel?*, encouraging them to write spontaneously and without pause for thought. Tell them that they have five minutes to write and that you will cue them when they have a minute left. Sharing the writing or the writing process can be encouraged, but is best made optional in this context.

Breathing exercises

The breath is our life force and a marker of our internal rhythm. In yoga when movements are done to the rhythm of the breath we can experience flow, a feeling which we can also achieve in writing. Generally we don't notice the breath until we are tense and we hold it or if we have a cold. These exercises are meant to bring awareness.

Ask the group to close their eyes, place their hands on their thighs and take three deep breaths in and out. Suggest that they imagine their bodies outlined in pencil, and to use the breath to fill this outline.

While their eyes are still closed, ask them to breathe at a comfortable pace with their hands on their bellies to feel the breath in this part of the body. Then ask them to move their hands to their kidneys, ribs and chests to feel the breath moving through them.

Ask the group to take a few breaths in and out, keeping their eyes closed. Then ask them to breath inwards for two counts as you count *one, two,* then to hold the breath for another two counts. As they breathe out, ask the students to lengthen their breath by breathing out to four counts as you count *one, two, three, four.* Do this three times.

Ask them to stand up and shake out their hands, arms, feet and legs.

Main writing exercise

When we are conscious of the breath, we are present in the body so this is a good moment to enable the students to access memories with a strong physical impression.

Ask them to close their eyes and take three deep breaths. Lead them on a guided meditation to access a strong sensual memory (Adams, *Journal to the self*, pp. 94–101.) This might include looking at a photo album or walking through a portrait gallery devoted to them, or using Adams's idea of imagining a movie screen of memories. The idea is to allow the students time for the memories to float by until one stands out. Encourage them to draw on all five senses to harness the sensual power of the memory. Allow seven to ten minutes writing time, then invite them to read or describe the experience of writing this piece.

Silent meditation

The workshop ends with a few minutes of silent meditation in which the students are asked to check in with their posture, notice their breath and observe if the mind is busy. It is a time to see if it is possible to shift the awareness from thinking to being.

End by encouraging any comments or questions and repeat the opening Om chant three times.

Conclusion

By doing yoga and writing exercises together, the body can relax, allowing space for the mind to unwind. In this safe and open environment, creativity can flourish and writing can flow freely.

Contributor: Beverly Frydman
The name Beverly was chosen for me because a girl named Beverly was kind to my mother, a newly-arrived, eight-year-old immigrant to the United States. I write journals in black and white marbled notebooks bought in American supermarkets. When I'm not writing I like to do yoga. I recommend *Bringing yoga to life* by Donna Farhi. Ask me if you need information on ice cream. I can't help you with horror movies. You'd never have known if I hadn't told you that I once had a pet skunk.

13

Suasoria: arguing for and against a proposition

Introduction

Arguing on both sides of the question is an exercise that goes back to Ancient Greece, and to the rhetorical schools of the early Roman empire. The Romans practised *controversiae*, where you were given the facts of a particularly knotty legal case and then had to devise arguments for one side and the other, and *suasoriae*, where you had to argue for and against a particular course of action. The suasoria was successfully revived during the Renaissance as an educational exercise. Queen Elizabeth I developed her rhetorical abilities by practising suasoriae – so did Shakespeare. The potent influence of this training can be seen in plays like *Julius Caesar*.

The suasoria, as a written exercise, can be practised at many different levels and with different age groups. It develops students' ability to think flexibly and to argue forcibly, lucidly and economically. It is excellent, practical training for many fields of work – journalism, legal practice, the civil service, and business – and students appreciate its applicability and engagement with real and pressing issues. For those pursuing creative writing as a potential career, it is also good training in developing professional detachment: an ability to gather material and write a polemically vibrant piece from a point of view that is distinct from the writer's own.

The exercise

Students are given a proposition, a statement that can be met with a 'yes' or 'no' answer. Examples of propositions that I have used with classes in the past include: 'It should be mandatory for all citizens to hold national identity cards'; 'Marriage should be encouraged by the State'; 'Addicted to unsustainable energy use, the Western world will fail to combat catastrophic climate change'; 'The UK's current voting system in general elections is a democratic and effective system of representation that should not be changed.'

The exercise is to argue in 800 words for the proposition and then in 800 words against it. Students should be instructed that this is not an imagined verbal speech, but a written task, and that they should therefore *not* attempt to inhabit a persona (to argue for State support of marriage, say, as a born-again Christian, and against it as a bitter divorcee). They should *not* supply an introduction or conclusion, balancing the merits of one position against the other, or indicate their 'real life' view, but simply put the most convincing case, on one side of the question and then the other, with maximum effectiveness. After reading it, the lecturer should not know which side the student actually favours: the general reader should be convinced, in turn, by the arguments for the proposition and then the arguments against it.

Students should be encouraged to do some research via the Internet and other resources in order to consider fully the evidence – statistical or otherwise – and possible lines of argument on either side. I ask for all sources to be footnoted, so that they can be checked. It's useful to tell the students before they begin that prior knowledge about the topic under debate is unimportant and that there is no 'right' and 'wrong' line of argument. Two different students, might, for example, argue for and against identity cards using completely different but equally compelling approaches. I encourage students to plan their argumentative strategy and structure closely, paragraph by paragraph, and to revise the wording minutely until they feel it is as convincing as they can possibly make it. I also encourage them to try out (verbally) different points on friends or classmates and thus to try to imagine how members of a diverse audience might respond to their lines of argument.

Younger or less able students could be introduced to the exercise by being given an example of a piece of writing, such as a newspaper leader, that takes the form of a suasoria and analysing it before attempting one of their own.

The objective

Writing a suasoria is a useful exercise for many reasons. It invites the writer to inhabit, successively, two opposing viewpoints on a single issue. To complete the task successfully s/he needs to engage in research, abandon temporarily any attachment to personally-held views, and objectively make the most forcible, lucid, and persuasive case first for one side, and then the other. The task also develops the skill of writing economically and thinking ahead about structure and audience response. Students learn to edit their own prose for maximum rhetorical impact: to revise individual sentences until they make the argument as punchy as possible.

After completing this relatively compact piece of work, for which I normally allow around three weeks (though it could be completed in a much briefer period), students have usually developed their professionalism about editing their own writing.

It also helps enhance their awareness of the rhetorical qualities of prose generally, and how these can be weakened – by rambling, unfocused sentences – or strengthened – by tight, precise, attention-grabbing writing. Students often report, as a side-effect, that they 'read newspapers differently', becoming highly aware of viewpoint and the author's rhetorical strategies.

In a sense, all writing is a form of persuasion, in that it seeks to make the reader read on. The suasoria allows students to experiment with the tools of persuasion in a journalistic fashion, but the effects of this exercise often rub off positively on their work in other academic and creative forms.

Contributor: Sara Lodge
My name is Sara J. Lodge – the 'J' stands for Jane, which was my grandmother's name. I write non-fiction, fiction, literary journalism and political speeches – but only for causes that move me. I recommend *The elements of style* by William Strunk Jr. and E.B. White. When I'm not writing, I like to paint. Ask me if you need information on speechwriting, wine, or nineteenth-century literature. I can't help you with sport, rodents, or your tax form. If I didn't tell you, you'd never know that I also work as an election monitor in the Caribbean and South America.

14

The (bridal) shop of ideas: shortcuts to inspiration

Introduction
There comes a time in most Q&A sessions when a student will ask, 'Where do you get your ideas from?' I often wish I could say, 'From a little shop on the high street, where an old lady dispenses ideas over the counter.' But, sadly, this wouldn't be true. Instead, I tell my students that their ideas will come from them, as writers. That what's required is dipping into the well of the subconscious, together with the development of a writer's antennae and the placing of their backsides on the seat, i.e. a marriage between hard graft and an openness to receive. This is the cue for long faces: especially if students have an assignment to deliver on time. So, I'll introduce them to these short cuts.

The exercise
I provide them with the handout below to stimulate class discussion. I then set the task of producing First Lines at the rate of one per day as preparation for the next meeting. I encourage them to have fun, to be bold, and even outrageous.

The following week they bring their seven lines to the class. These are distributed randomly so that students can use a donated First Line as a prompt for focused freewrite during the session.

They then have the other exercises on the handout as a future resource. Alternatively, any of the other exercises are easily adapted for class or online use.

The bridal shop of ideas

SOMETHING OLD

Go through your workbooks, notebooks, exercises and see if there's anything which grabs. Is there anything which could be developed? Freewrite, mind map, etc. Does it excite you?

SOMETHING NEW

Make keeping a writer's notebook/journal a daily habit. Use a watch or clock and say 'I'm going to write anything at all for fifteen minutes.' Start and don't stop until time is up. Go with first thoughts.

Find prompts from books/websites, etc. Use photographs, collect postcards from art galleries. Freewrite for twenty minutes. Anything worth developing?

Go on location with your notebook. Sit in a café or art gallery. Write and write. Note things that catch the eye, snippets of conversation, anything and everything: brief character descriptions, sketches of people out and about. What is their story? Where might they be going? About to do? What if? What if? What if?

Have a go at writing first lines:

First lines

Look at famous first lines from classic novels and appreciate what these writers have achieved. Next, buy a small notebook in which to write your own – totally random – first lines. One line a day for a month. By the end of which you will have thirty possible beginnings! The only rule is to go for a cracking first line.

Your first lines can remain as stuff in a notebook or be developed. Try selecting five first lines and have a go at continuing each by writing the next one hundred words. Next, decide which one you think has got 'legs'. Develop into a story. The rest can be kept for later. Continue writing first lines whenever you like. You are collecting stock for your very own shop of ideas.

SOMETHING BORROWED

Take a collection of short stories and choose one a random. Copy the first line of that short story onto a new piece of paper. This is now a first line prompt for a focused freewrite of twenty minutes. At the end, cross off that borrowed first line, which you may not keep/use as that would be plagiarism. Next, cast a critical eye over the freewriting. Is there enough raw material for a story? A start? A new prompt? The same can be done with poetry.

Borrow first lines only. These contain the essence of a story or poem. This is the line which the author has honed until it's spot on. It provides an excellent springboard into your own writing.

SOMETHING BLUE

Sex! Don't forget the loins. A poet needs to employ the head, the heart and the loins. Many, new to writing, forget (or are unaware of) the loins. Some might overdo the head, producing writing which is lofty, polemic, or intellectualised. Some might overdo the heart, producing text that is emotive, gushing, or melodramatic.

What is often called for is the loins. The loins are the sensuous appetite. The loins are grounded, visceral, employ the concrete and all the senses: the seat of analogy and metaphor, e.g. what does this look like, sound like, smell like, taste like? What does it remind me of?

The loins may or may not include sex, gore or violence. Beware being gratuitous. A light touch and balance are required. But a dash adds the spice of life to any tale. So, go through your freewrites, First Line or developed ideas and see where you can add that spice to your writing.

The objective

The main objective is to enable students to demonstrate that the best ideas can come from their own imaginings, subconscious, and the physical act of writing. From a lecturer's point of view, it's a quick way to kick start creativity, plus a reminder to students that writing can and should be fun.

Contributor: Rosemary Dun

My last name is the Scottish spelling of a Celtic word. I'm forever telling people that Dun has one 'n'. A cashier at my local bank once asked, 'Are you sure?' I write contemporary women's novels, short stories, poetry. I recommend *Write a blockbuster and get it published* by Helen Corner and Lee Weatherly. When I'm not writing, I co-host Big Mouth Cabaret. Ask me if you need information on *Columbo*. I can't help you with the inner workings of a computer programme. If I didn't tell you, you'd never know that I once had a pet jackdaw.

15

Using place in prose

Introduction

Place is a powerful and effective means for story-writing that can be developed at any point in the generation of a text, from inception to final drafting. As with character, it is also an aspect of fiction to which most people have a developed relationship, both personally and through reading, regardless of writing experience. As such, these exercises can and have been adapted to any level of proficiency, from novice first-year undergraduate to experienced postgraduate, though I have pitched the following outline at its most basic level. It should take two hours if photocopies are handed out and read prior to the class. I have combined life-writing, collaborative fiction writing, small and whole group discussion and close reading.

Materials

1. Photocopies of contrasting place descriptions: e.g. Baskerville Hall in Conan Doyle's *The Hound of the Baskervilles*; Holly Golightly's flat in Capote's *Breakfast at Tiffany's*.
2. Photocopies of descriptions of contrasting places within one novel: e.g. Lowood boarding school and Thornfield Hall in Charlotte Brontë's *Jane Eyre*.
3. A photocopied list of atmospheric local place names.

The exercises

PLACES ARE PERSONAL

The lecturer opens by describing a place where a personally emotive event happened to them: e.g. hearing bad news, falling in love, finding peace. Descriptive elements should suggest both the mood and event – weather, colours, adjectives, background activity, etc. – but the mood and event should not themselves be disclosed. Students are then invited to make guesses about these before being asked to choose their own places for a similar activity they are to conduct.

Students are asked to create a written piece describing the place as if they were a passive observer, communicating mood and event through choice of word, not through telling the story or their emotions.

The finished pieces are read out, each in turn, working in groups of three or four. As each student finishes, the rest of their group make guesses about the mood and, if possible, the event.

FICTIONAL PLACES ARE PERSONALISED (1)

The class is asked to contribute the aspects of the descriptions that students have just heard which have been found to be most effective in communicating mood. The lecturer – or a nominated student – writes up these aspects on one half of a board.

Students are asked to suggest well-known fictional places: e.g. Hogwarts, Wuthering Heights, Macondo. The lecturer – or student – writes these up on the other half of the board.

Students then discuss whether the first list reflects the effectiveness of places on the second list or not and if other aspects need to be added.

FICTIONAL PLACES ARE PERSONALISED (2)
Students are divided into groups of three or four. Using knowledge already developed during class, the groups analyse the first two photocopied texts and discuss:
1. what the writer has chosen to focus on and why;
2. what relationship exists between character and place;
3. what the description reveals or suggests about the story;
4. which each student prefers and why.
A representative from each group feeds back to the whole class and the lecturer offers points of interest and conflict to the class for discussion. A break can follow, if required.

A TALE OF TWO PLACES
Students are invited to suggest to the class contrasting places within one book, such as The Shire and Mordor, Wuthering Heights and Thrushcross Grange. The lecturer writes these on the board.

Students are then asked to discuss the effects of contrasting places in terms of plot, character, theme and mood.

Working in groups of three or four, they are asked to analyse the second set of photocopies by considering how these places are contrasted and what effects the contrast creates.

Representatives from each group feed back to the whole class.

Students then work in pairs, first choosing two places with contrasting names from the list of place names. Using the two places, they will then develop a story – either writing in full or in note form, depending on the time allowance – to present to the class. The story should focus on a character from one place visiting the other and being transformed in some way. Ask students to include all the knowledge from the session – thematic development, character description, etc.

The class concludes with students presenting their pieces to the rest of the group – with feedback, if time permits. Alternatively, the pieces can be completed as homework.

The objective
Aside from the acquisition and/or refreshment of writing skills directly relating to place, this exercise enables students to create mood, impart information and develop theme through the careful and subtle use of detail. This skill set can be applied to other areas of creative writing and, in turn, the lesson can be used to re-enforce learning objectives running throughout a module.

In addition, at more advanced levels, these exercises also lend themselves to discussion utilising tools gained from critical theory, such as ecocriticism and cultural geography. This develops the idea of place as an active force in plotting, rather than simply a background, through developing an understanding of the influence exerted on characters by place.

Contributor: Andy Thatcher
My name is Andy Thatcher. Because I was a hyperactive child, I was nicknamed Akii-Bua, after a Ugandan hurdler. I write contemporary long fiction and haiku. I like watching tornado footage on YouTube. I recommend that you read Paul Dawson's *Creative writing and the new humanities.* Ask me if you need information on shamanism or Andy Warhol. I can't help you with ironing or team sports. If I didn't tell you, you'd never know that I'm the great-grandson of the chief steward on HMS Lusitania, who went down with his ship when it was torpedoed by a German submarine.

16

Formal verse for the faint-hearted

Introduction
To describe the characteristics of a given form may be done
with ease; the challenge for the lecturer is most often to
convince students of their value. The exercises below,
therefore, aim not to introduce mechanical processes, but to
demonstrate how the form words take affects their content.

Exercise 1: the pantoum
I find that a useful way to engage students is to begin with the
pantoum. Following its brief burst of European popularity in
the nineteenth century, this Malayan form has never been much
more than a curio for occasional experimentation. However, its
form lends itself well to collaborative participation. Written in
quatrains rhymed ABAB, the second and fourth lines of each
stanza become the first and third of the next; the final stanza is
completed by the third line of the first becoming its second and
the first line of the poem being repeated as the final line. It is fun
to write these with groups of any size in the manner of a game
of consequences, writing a line and passing it on; after the first
stanza, the pattern of repetition will move the poem forward,
and there is also the advantage that length is open-ended, so
that it can be adjusted depending on the class dynamic.

Whilst poems produced this way almost always have
an element of nonsense, this in itself makes for valuable
insights into the effect that a particular form may have.
Regardless of content, repetition and the return to the

poem's beginning in its conclusion have a tangible effect on the reader. The explicit sense of closure it provides causes the reader to impose meaning even where there may not be any. In addition, and in concert with the repetition, the pantoum is a discrete form that pulls against the development of thought or action; however light-hearted the subject may be, there is always a tangible sense of constraint, which can often lead to a perceptible tension between humour and threat in content and form.

Exercise 2: the sonnet

Once the active role of form in creating meaning for the reader has been established and students have had the opportunity to explore the potential of the pantoum for themselves, the sonnet – by virtue of both its heritage and generic distinctiveness – offers an appropriate next step. On the face of it, the sonnet shouldn't be that hard; after all, the ground rules are pretty clear.

A sonnet has fourteen lines, is generally in iambic pentameter (or with some slight variation thereof), and traditionally follows one of three rhyme schemes: the Petrarchan (ABBA ABBA CDECDE – the rhyme of these final six lines may be varied); the Shakespearean (ABAB CDCD EFEF GG); the Spenserean (ABAB BCBC CDCD EE). If you wish to explore this at length, providing a list of rhyme words and asking students to fill in the blank lines can lead to rewarding discussions on the versatility of both metre and rhyme.

However, in looking at examples from the Renaissance to the present – Don Paterson's *101 sonnets* offers a particularly good collection, and has an introduction that every would-be sonneteer should read – it becomes apparent that rhyme, metre and even length may be manipulated for effect. Once this near-infinite flexibility has been recognised, there is less temptation to slip into the traps of loading lines with redundant words to fill an arbitrary quota of jog-trot iambs or torturing natural syntax into submission in order to reach a tired rhyme on cue. Instead, it allows students to think of the sonnet as a structure for advancing an argument, placing content at the heart of the process. For, in contrast to the halting, recursive nature of the pantoum, the sonnet has long been established as the ideal form to articulate concise argument.

Whilst the idea that, say, the English sonnet breaks neatly into a quatrain that establishes a thesis, a second that presents the antithesis, and a sestet in which they are synthesised, is as debateable as any other rule-of-thumb we may apply to the form, it is nonetheless a fruitful approach to suggest an argumentative structure as a way of approaching the sonnet.

In order to keep this easily manageable for novices, I have found that breaking the process into couplets is an effective, non-threatening way of guiding students through the process. First, students should think of a question to address, whether it is one of the Big Questions of love, life and death which have perplexed poets throughout the centuries, or simply whether to get up with the alarm on a cold, wet morning. After this, they should write two lines – disregarding questions of length or rhyme – on each of the following points:

State the predicament. This will most likely involve a *how* or *why* at some point.

What may happen if they make one decision?

What will happen if they do the opposite?

What will happen if they do nothing?

Reflecting on these options, which would they ideally take and why?

What would be the ultimate benefit?

What, in either specific or more general terms, have they gained from thinking this problem through?

Even the most clumsy results at this stage reveal the usefulness of the sonnet's characteristics: the lens it provides through which to view a question; its encouragement to focus on essentials and precisely balance options; its inherent, yet indefinable 'rightness' in employing the 'turn' at the start of the sestet as a point at which one moves towards a conclusion.

The objective

Following this, students can revise what they have written, thinking about lexis, imagery and, if they like, more formal metrical concerns. However, in many ways the important business has been done, and what is often initially perceived by students to be a restrictive form has been demonstrated to be a perfect vehicle for the exploration of personal and/or universal concerns in one's own distinctive individual voice.

Contributor: Paul Hardwick

Most people call me Oz, after Ozymandias the owl on 70s television show *Ace of wands*, and this is the name I use for poetry, music, photography and journalism. I'm in charge of programmes in English and Writing at Leeds Trinity University College in northern England. I recommend *The making of a poem* by Mark Strand and Eavan Boland. When I'm not writing, I like messing about on acoustic stringed instruments. I'm always happy to talk about English misericords or Richard Brautigan. I'm hopeless with computers and forget acronyms. If I didn't tell you, you'd never know I once played at Glastonbury Festival.

17

Stylistic modelling: creative engagement with word classes and syntax

Introduction
Grammar can be an off-putting topic for students and teachers alike. Many students feel intimidated and confused by the terminology, while teachers might dread grinding through the technicalities of language use. And yet a strong grasp of the language choices available can make all the difference when it comes to crafting something brilliant.

This exercise has been developed following Dorothea Brande's advice 'On Imitation' in *Becoming a writer* (p.83). She recommends a close mapping of style as a way to refresh one's own writing. At first students may feel that such plodding mimicry is the opposite of creativity. But they will find they can produce stunning effects of their own through borrowing the language structures of another author – sometimes even better than the original!

The exercise
Encourage students to begin by choosing a paragraph from an author they admire. It is best to start with more recent writing as a model – diving straight into Charles Dickens or Jane Austen can prove quite a challenge, though highly instructive when compared to modern works. It's also best to pick prose rather than poetry, but it doesn't have to be fiction.

ANALYSIS

The first step is to identify the word classes used in the model. It's helpful to use a different colour to highlight examples from each word class. Then you end up with a colour map of the model's distinctive style. The key pedagogical issue here is to support students in moving from identifying features of language use to exploring effects that are created for the reader or audience. A 'fingerprint' of style will begin to emerge, and this can be discussed in relation to genre and the author's designs on the reader. You may find it easier to make three different maps of any text, as outlined in the three paragraphs below.

How does the use of articles or determiners contribute to the overall feel of the writing – the atmosphere, the reader's expectations? Taken together, are the nouns in this passage predominantly concrete or abstract, or is there an even mix? Are there any extended noun phrases? How are these constructed – what role is played by adjectives, for example? How do noun phrases help to shape the overall rhythm?

Move on to verbs, focusing on tense and person, subjects and objects, transitives and intransitives, active and passive voice. As above, how do adverbials affect the rhythm and the reader's experience of this scene?

Finally: punctuation and sentence structure. In a piece of action writing, the sentences may be quite short and some of them may be minor sentences. The interruption of a clause by another statement through hyphens, brackets or commas may help to convey a particular attitude or a character's state of mind. How might the same information have been conveyed using different sentence lengths and punctuation marks?

All the way through the analysis, keep reminding students to focus on the function of a word rather than its type. 'Deep' is most familiar to us as an adjective, so students may be confused to encounter it in 'the briny deep'. Keep asking: what is this word's job in the sentence? What kind of information is it carrying?

MODELLING
This stage of the exercise can be incorporated along the way in small steps, as a way of consolidating each of the three areas of language use covered in the analysis. The analytic work is thereby relieved by tackling the same issues from a creative angle. At the end, modelling can be completed as a full activity in its own right, leading into a workshop if desired.

There are two options here: parody and pastiche. Parody can be easier, because there is less temptation to get distracted by copying the theme. The student selects a very different and disjunct theme through which to apply the chosen author's style. One of my students took a passage from H.P. Lovecraft and used it to describe the experience of having to change endless nappies in the middle of the night. Or the clipped sentences of an action thriller may be applied to a banal everyday situation such as the supermarket checkout. For pastiche, students will need to select a subject matter that is more suited to the original author's language choices.

Timing and resources
The whole process, including a workshop session, can be spread over four two-hour sessions. But any one of the three analysis stages may be incorporated into a single

session, if your intention is to sharpen students' awareness of a particular feature of language use, such as adjectives or adverbials, or the crafting of prose in a particular genre, such as action thrillers, science fiction or more literary scene setting.

David Crystal's *Making sense of grammar* and *Rediscover grammar* are useful background reading, as are the grammar sections of the University of Ottawa Hypergrammar and Purdue Online Writing Lab. However, most resources in this area will go into more detail than is directly useful for creative writing purposes. Students will need guidance in selecting and working with key information on word classes so as not to get bogged down in technicalities.

The objective

Creative writing classes often contain students who have studied language at an advanced level alongside those who have had little or no formal teaching of grammar at all. The first group can benefit from looking beyond technicalities to explore authorial choices and effects created for the reader. The second will need their confidence building, bringing their intuitive knowledge of grammar to the surface.

The analysis stages can be worth the effort, for students and teachers alike: closely modelled parodies can be devastating and hilarious, while pastiche work can be stunning and surprising.

Students can also make important discoveries about how closely style and content are wedded in good writing. In some cases the shape of a sentence can almost function as a performance of its message. Sometimes it can be quite difficult to break into another author's style and borrow their sentence shapes for a different purpose. This too is instructive: demonstrating how the writing has been crafted to say just what the author wanted it to and nothing else.

Contributor: Katy Price
My full name is Katharine Emma. I've been known as Katie, Kate and Katy. I write poetry and texts for performance with music – see katyprice.wordpress.com. I recommend *Writing: self and reflexivity* by Celia Hunt and Fiona Sampson. When I'm not writing, I sleep late, eat salad, ride my bike and practise Aikido. Ask me about making dresses out of comics. I can't help you aboard ship. If I didn't tell you, you'd never know that I worked in a homeless hostel before going away to uni.

18

Working with desire to build plot

Introduction

It was Kurt Vonnegut's stated belief that characters must exhibit and act on desires from the word go, even those suffering the most dire case of existential ennui (Hayman et al. (eds.) 'The art of fiction no. 64: Kurt Vonnegut', *Paris Review*). Though I'm often at odds with Vonnegut's no-nonsense bluntness, I fully agree with him here. Carefully working with desire provides the backbone of any plot – however minor its role in a piece – through bringing characters into conflict with one another, their environment and themselves. Just as importantly, through acting on desire, or not, the reader gets to witness characters as living things, not static figures.

This workshop plan is pitched at beginner to intermediate writers. It can take between one and two hours, depending on how much time is given to discussion and creative work and combines personal and collaborative fiction writing, small and whole group discussion, and close reading.

Materials

1. Photocopies of folk tales so that the class can be split into groups of no more than four, with each group reading a different story. I use those found in any of the Barefoot Books collections (e.g. *The Barefoot book of animal tales*) as they are short, clear and well told.
2. One set of character cards per group. These can be pre-bought (e.g. Cluedo cards), a set of photos,

evocative names, or outline characters (e.g. Anais Patel: policewoman by day, karaoke queen by night). If students have been building characters in a previous lesson, this is a good opportunity to recycle previous material.
3. A list of random objects, e.g. park bench, urn of ashes, a jar of dead bats, crutches.

The exercises

EVERYBODY WANTS TO RULE THE WORLD

The lecturer begins by describing a selection of his or her desires, such as wanting a cup of tea, wanting to go back to bed, wanting the students to become published writers, wanting global recognition and riches, wanting to go tornado chasing. I find it best to think of a range of realistic and unrealistic desires, selfish and selfless desires, safe and dangerous desires.

The class is split into groups of three to five students. Each group is asked to come up with as many desires as possible – a 'volunteer' or the lecturer then writes these up on the board.

The whole class discusses where acting on a selection of these desires might lead – the lecturer looks to elicit 'conflict' as an answer. The inquiry subsequently shifts to which conflicts these desires might lead to.

CONFLICT AND DESIRE IN FOLK TALES

Returning to the small groups, each one is given enough photocopies of one folk tale for a copy per person. After reading through, groups are asked to discuss which desires operate in each story, how they bring about conflict, how the desire is resolved – or not – by the end and the role that desire plays in developing plot and character.

The responses are fed back to the whole class, with any new kinds of desire being added to the list on the board. The lecturer guides the class to consider what kinds of conflict are encountered in these stories: e.g. inner conflict, life-or-death conflict, personality conflict, conflict of interests, cultural conflict, etc.

If required, build in a short break at this point.

CREATIVE ACTIVITY

The small groups are given a set time (I allow forty minutes) to come up with a completed story to present to the class that will take less than five minutes to perform. Each group is given the same set of character cards and a list of random objects.

The following instructions may be handed out or written on the board:

1. Individually, choose a character card and create a series of desires for that character.
2. Present your character to the rest of your group.
3. Collectively, decide on one character as a primary character and one object from the list to include in the story.
4. Discuss how the primary character's desires might bring them into conflict with their environment, themselves and the desires of the other characters your group has developed.
5. Choose one primary desire for your primary character.
6. Develop a story in which that desire reaches resolution by the end. Include the other characters and the object.
7. Present the story as you wish.

Students should present pieces to the class by the end of the lesson, receiving feedback from peers and lecturer.

The objective
This workshop provides a way of thinking about the relationship between character and plot without prescriptively providing a formula. Its objective is to reveal, first through discussion, then through experimentation, the centrality of desire and conflict to the experience of fiction and to present a raised awareness of that centrality as key to developing strong work, from inception to final draft editing.

Contributor: Andy Thatcher
My name is Andy Thatcher and, no, I'm no relation – though my nickname at school was 'Maggie'. I write contemporary fiction and haiku and am dabbling in the gothic short story. I recommend M.M. Bakhtin's *Problems of Dostoevsky's poetics* for its dissection of free indirect speech. I love horse chestnut trees, National Trust tea-rooms and West African blues. Ask me if you need information on acid house or volcanoes. I can't help you with internet routers or smartphones. You'd never guess that I once pushed Rolf Harris's trolley at Gatwick Airport. He drew me a Rolfaroo.

19

Poetry out loud: a performance poetry workshop

Introduction
Performance poetry is a performing arts discipline that encompasses the skills required for theatre, standup comedy, and live music.

It benefits from being taught in a performance space where fellow students and lecturers can give feedback on performance/stage technique/rhythm/content and so on. It is primarily for the stage, though written on the page, so needs to be workshopped aloud, live, and in front of an audience of peers.

In common with standup comedy, a performance poet may plan a set of say, five, ten or fifteen minutes, with a beginning, middle and end that make it very similar to the three-act structure of a play. There will also be links between poems for coherence and through lines such as themes and subject matter. In common with theatre, the performance poet considers the voice and body as instruments and might use theatre warm-up techniques.

However, unlike theatre, performance poetry never has a fourth wall, but is more like standup comedy in that it engages directly with the audience. It also has similarities to a music set as applause is given at the end of each poem. While this very brief overview reveals commonalities, overlaps and differences, it is a specific art form.

Performance poetry is also not the same as a poetry reading. At a reading, it's the words that are most important, with the poet's delivery, however good or bad, being secondary. Performance poetry, however, relies on both performance and poem equally. Going further, I would maintain that performance poetry is the fusion between poem and persona. What the audience respond to is not just the word, not just the performance, but also the persona of the poet.

Philip Norton, slam poet and co-editor of *Short fuse: the global anthology of new fusion poets*, reminds us that performance poetry is accessible and – above all – not boring. After all, an audience has come along and paid for a night's entertainment. At best it is moving and inspiring, connecting with an audience so that they go away thinking about it, much as they would at the end of a good play or film.

The exercise: poetry swap shop

It's helpful to students if you explain that while notation on a musical score enables a musician to perform a song, by the same token, punctuation, the use of white spaces, stanza length and line breaks are essential for the performance poet.

Much as page poetry helps train the eye, so performance poetry helps train the ear. Hearing our own work read by someone else is a good test of how well it is working and brings a wholly different perspective which aids the editing process.

Ask your students in advance to bring two copies of one poem for workshopping. This poem should take no longer than four minutes to read.

In pairs, the students find a space where they can stand facing one another. One student reads the other's poem out loud while the author of the poem listens in silence.

After the reading, they both take five minutes to make notes using the following handout questionnaires:

Performance poetry feedback
PERFORMER/READER
1. Was the poem easy to read?
2. How about rhythm? Scansion? Musicality?
3. Were there any lines which were 'clunky'? Any words or phrases you stumbled over? Feel free to make notes on the poem.
4. Did it have meaning? Was it accessible?
5. Did it entertain?
6. What did you like?
7. What were you not so keen on?
8. Anything else?

LISTENER/POET
1. What was the experience like for you?
2. What did you notice?
3. Did your poem work?
4. Did it have the same rhythm and emphases as when you perform it? If not, why not?
5. Did it have meaning? Make sense?
6. Did it say what you wanted it to say?
7. Anything else?

The performer gives her/his notes to the listener, who should not look at them until the whole exercise is at an end.

They then swap roles and the exercise is repeated as above. After twenty minutes, they will have performed and listened and have notes from their listener plus their own notes for reference.

You can then ask the whole group to reform to share experiences and any surprises. This should take about thirty minutes in all.

As well as the experience and discussion to think about, the students now have the basis for another edit of their own poems. Ask them to bring the edited versions to the following week's class for reading/performing to the whole class and discussion on the changes made.

The objective
To enable critique and editing as a result of students listening to how their words translate from the page to being spoken out loud by somebody else. Just as page poetry needs to be laid out carefully on the page to lead the reader's eye around the poem, so a performance poem needs to be equally well-written to enable it to be interpreted out loud. This exercise aids with critique and editing.

I always advise my performance poetry students to hone their skills and their poetry by signing up for open mic slots and slam poetry competitions. There is a poetry circuit, just as there are standup comedy and music circuits, so taking part could become an extension exercise.

Contributor: Rosemary Dun
My middle name is Anne. My mother was going to name me after her best friend Mary, but then my initials would have been M.A.D.! I recommend John Whitworth's *Writing*

Poetry. I can't help you with cooking – I'm rubbish. Not many people know that I am a Stroud Football Poet or that I have football poems published in school textbooks in Germany, Estonia and Finland.

20

Using Web 2.0 in the creative writing workshop: blogs and wikis

Introduction
Over the last ten years the Internet has revolutionised the way we communicate and share information. This has been especially so since the birth of the second generation web page, or Web 2.0, as it has become known, which allows a more interactive, user-centred environment. It is on the back of Web 2.0 that blogs and wikis have become prominent on the Web.

In fact, both are fairly simple concepts: a blog is simply a web log, either recorded individually or by a 'community' of some kind; a wiki is an editable web page, normally again used by a 'community' of users. An example of a wiki would be *Wikipedia* that allows its users to edit its own entries.

Access to blogs and wikis has significantly improved across schools, colleges and universities as they have become embedded within virtual learning environments. So much so, that for many lecturers, they can now be incorporated into the ongoing running of a creative writing workshop. It's something I've been doing for some time now, and I want to share two possible activities with you. The only resource needed is access to a workshop blog for lecturer and students.

1. A blog-based activity
'Story chain' is an activity that is especially suited to an asynchronous electronic environment such as a blog. In

this activity, the task is completed in the students' own time, outside of the workshop.

THE EXERCISE

A story is begun by the lecturer, using no more than one hundred words. This is posted up on the blog. In their own time, students then read the entry, furthering the story with their own piece (again, no more than one hundred words). The blog will ensure these entries are recorded sequentially, mirroring the order in which the students add their pieces to the ongoing story chain.

Since the activity takes place outside of the workshop, it can be done over several days. This is a good exercise for first-year undergraduates but can be used more generally as an introductory session on any course.

THE OBJECTIVE

The exercise is a good ice-breaker. It is especially good for introducing new students to the – often daunting – experience of being read by their peers. It is also good for building camaraderie and trust across a workshop.

In terms of technique, the different entries can then be examined in the workshop itself, the lecturer using the blog to encourage debate about various aspects of creative practice, including plot, characterisation and creativity.

2. Editing and revision using a wiki

The creative writing workshop can be successfully extended by the use of wikis. Wikis are editable web pages that allow the personalised tracking of any changes done to that page. This means they are perfect at capturing any editing done to creative writing, for instance.

THE EXERCISE

In this task the students are paired up. The first (assigned as *writer*) produces a short story outside the face-to-face group workshop. The second student (assigned as *editor*) then edits the story as best he or she can to a 'publishable' standard, again outside the workshop. This might include removing spelling mistakes, but could also include the rewriting of sentences, and the addition or removal of words and phrases. In short, anything goes. Since the activity of both *writer* and *editor* takes place in their own time, it can be done over several days.

The wiki ensures that both versions of the story are preserved as nothing is lost. The decisions of both *writer* and *editor* can then be examined by the whole group.

THE OBJECTIVE

The exercise is especially good at introducing students to the importance of revision and editing. By exploring the relationship between *writing* and *editing* on the wiki, the exercise highlights the benefits as well as issues and tensions in this process. For the *editor*, it briefly empowers the student in a way they may be unused to. For the *writer*, it introduces the concept of being read and critiqued by someone else, which can be uncomfortable. At the end of the workshop, the students should have a clear idea about why the editing of their own writing is so important and the techniques needed to go about this process.

Contributor: Spencer Jordan
My full name is Spencer Kenneth Jordan. The middle name comes from my grandfather who was killed in the Second World War. He was a rear-gunner in an American

Liberator bomber. I write mainly historical fiction, but also short stories. Ask me if you'd like someone to help put up a tent. I can't help you with DIY or car maintenance. If I didn't tell you you'd never know that I'd gone hiking in the Himalayas.

21

Food writing: mobilising the five senses and personal memories

Introduction

Food features in fiction and non-fiction writing. Food writing often combines various kinds of narratives, so that a restaurant review can include autobiographical memoir, travel writing and a chef's biography alongside menu information. Today, food writing is increasingly concerned with important social issues such as personal health and environmental sustainability.

This wide range of focus means that food writing can be useful in various writing courses, not just those focused on food writing itself. As students and lecturers can usually identify with what is being written about – the smell of a favourite meal, comfort food's solace, cooking and eating – food-based exercises can also assist in facilitating involvement in both the face-to-face and online workshop.

Fruit writing exercise

Timing: 10 to 30 minutes

This exercise requires a piece of whole or cut fruit for each writer and writing materials. The entire class can work with the same or different fruits, which can be provided by the lecturer or students. As tasting is not mandatory, food allergies and dislikes aren't problematic, but having students supply their own fruit reduces any potential problems in this regard and means this exercise can also be used in online instruction.

I either distribute or ask students to place their fruit in front of them, and to contemplate it silently for a full minute, trying to assess the fruit using just one of the five senses – which I usually prescribe, although not always. I then ask students to write a description of the fruit using just this one sense.

This exercise is then repeated, by focusing on another sense, with students again spending a minute observing their fruit before starting writing. I leave the way they approach this observation up to them and it can include tasting, if they wish. I usually allow about three minutes for writing, but vary this if I have more – or less – time. The only comment I make during the writing time is to urge students not to use clichés or other worn descriptions.

If I want to extend the exercise, I ask the students to add further single sense descriptions, or swap fruits and try the same or a different sense description.

This exercise can be used online but a variation, which works especially well in a face-to-face class, is to show an image of a piece of fruit and ask students to write a visual description of it. Then distribute pieces of this fruit and ask students to write descriptions using one or more of the other four senses. Specifying that students use their aural sense when describing their fruit really gets them to flex their descriptive muscles!

If time permits, I call for volunteers to read from their work. I lead the discussion to focus on which of the senses offer the most vivid, powerful or resonant descriptions, and why. As writers, the students can reflect on which senses they found the most useful, while as listeners they can identify what held their interest.

Comparing the single sense descriptions allows students to debate which senses offer the freshest descriptions of everyday items. To follow up, they can locate good (or poor) examples of writing about fruit. They can also outline a story, poem or article that their descriptions could fit into, or polish their piece to contribute to a collaborative 'fruit salad'.

Food memoir exercise
Timing: 10 minutes plus
The strong impression food makes upon us is used in this exercise to access a memory. It requires only writing materials and can be used in a face-to-face or synchronous online class.

I ask students to begin thinking about a favourite food or drink or one they especially dislike. I then ask them to write about what they find particularly pleasant or unpleasant about it. After two or three minutes, I ask them to stop writing and recall a vivid memory that this food or drink evokes. Then, to write about that memory, but without mentioning the food or drink by name.

I use the following prompts: Is this a favourite (or not) from your childhood or is this a taste from the recent past? Have your tastes changed? Does taste, scent/aroma, or colour play a particularly important part in this memory? Who and where does this food remind you of, and what is going on when you think about it?

This is an exercise that students often find quite absorbing and the time they spend writing can range from a few minutes to much longer. Readings can be shared in the class or pieces polished and presented or posted to the group at a later time.

Due to the link with personal memory, readers should volunteer to share their work, rather than be nominated. I ask listeners/readers to focus on attempting to guess the food being written about. Group discussion can then move on to how the food contributes to the vividness and authenticity of the memory being described. To help guide this discussion, I ask what effect omitting the food, or naming the item, would have on the text.

As a follow up exercise in class or as homework, I ask students to write a recipe to accompany the text, or to be included within it.

The objective

The objective of these exercises is to heighten students' responses to food and then assist them in harnessing these reactions to write without clichés and access untapped memories to use in their work. Due to our sensory relationship with food, these exercises are especially useful to help focus on taste and aroma, senses that are often overlooked by student writers.

Contributor: Donna Lee Brien

My name is Donna Lee Brien. I live on a small Australian sheep farm, 800 miles from my university. When not travelling or working online, I am working on a history of Australian food writers. My favourite writers for class use are Margaret Fulton, Marion Halligan, Elizabeth David, M.F.K. Fisher and Nigella Lawson. Please ask me if you need information about how clever sheep are, but not how to kill them. Although you might guess I'm a vegetarian, it is less obvious that I hate the taste of olives.

22

'Digital lyre': conducting an audio workshop

Introduction

Conducting a workshop using sound files provides an alternative to paper-based creative writing classes. It offers a change of pace for the students and also responds to some of the challenges of the traditional workshop.

First, it means less time spent passing around and shuffling copies. Somehow a course for which students produce a large proportion of the texts always seems to present logistical difficulties. Second, audio submission forestalls the students' attention to layout over language. My classes often have a justifiable interest in how the poem looks on the page, but their attention to typography can merge into less productive discussion about font, type colour, placement of the author's name, and other considerations that should be secondary to composition.

Audio submission can also minimise references to the author's intention for the work. Once the poem has been typed up, students tend to refer to the printed copy, not to their own or their classmates' responses, as authoritative. The sense of printed text as the final word can cause resistance to differing readings or valid critiques. Avoiding even this most basic form of publication helps to place the emphasis on the workshop as process.

The exercise

For an audio workshop, the lecturer and students need access to recording software and microphones. The course management software my university uses comes with a suite of voice tools, including a voice board that works much like a discussion board. Alternatively, students could record and then email sound files to a common email list. As for recording devices, many computers now have built-in microphones, and students can get even better sound quality using basic headsets with microphones. Even many mobile phones have a voice recorder as standard so, while quality may be variable, accessibility of sound recording equipment is not usually a problem.

In my course, this exercise takes the place of a round of traditional workshops, so each student composes a new poem to submit in audio format. They record their poems using home computers, share them with the group via email, then listen to their peers' work individually before coming to the group workshop.

As a variation, you might try having students pair up and ask each to make a recording of the other's poem, so that they hear their own writing in a new voice.

To prepare students for the assignment, I suggest to them that audio submission will encourage closer attention to sound, both as they compose their poems and as they comment to one another. I ask them to listen to each submitted work several times. I always suggest repeated reading of poems, but this assignment has the added benefit of making repetition necessary, simply because it is hard to catch everything the first time you listen to the poems. Students have to go back and play each recording a second or third time in order to develop an understanding of the work, a task that feels more challenging when they don't have the entire text in front of them.

I also ask students to jot down their responses, make note of words or phrases that stand out to them as well-chosen or problematic, write down a few phrases about how the rhythm of the poem feels, and characterise what kinds of sounds it uses (i.e. choppy, mellow, hissing, etc.). These directions give them some specific formal elements to comment on, which I hope will deepen their responses to the content of the poems. Finally, I ask them to bring their notes to class to guide discussion. These become the foundation of the in-class workshop, for which we would normally refer to the printed page. Each student usually brings a copy of his or her poem to read at the beginning of our discussion, but it also works well to have them leave all paper copies at home and play the audio recording again at the start.

The objective

The primary goal of this workshop is to encourage students to write with more attention to the sounds of language, whether those sounds come in the form of heightened rhythm, end and internal rhyme, or patterns of alliteration and assonance.

For some of my students, this focus produces poems that break away from their established subjects or techniques. Ideally, the recordings also require a more patient approach to the submitted poems through the need for repeated listening.

My aim is that, using the audio workshop, students let the content and the form of the work unfold over several encounters rather than demanding meaning on a first reading. In other words, I think this format has the possibility to teach, without seeming to teach, one of the most important techniques for reading, especially reading poetry.

Contributor: Stefanie Wortman
My name is Stefanie Wortman. I live in Columbia, Missouri, a college town and burgeoning documentary film centre. I write poetry, essays, and criticism. I recommend that you read Kenneth Koch's *Making your own days*. When I'm not writing, I like to knit sweaters or ride my bike. I know a bit about old movies, but I'm clueless about sports. You would probably never guess that I used to dream of becoming a stockbroker.

23

To You or not to You?
Using second person in prose

Introduction

Second person perspective poses a fascinating problem for a creative writing student – and for a creative writing lecturer. Many creative writing books warn against its usage and yet there are some wonderful examples of texts in which the success of the story is largely down to the use of this unusual form of address.

It is these texts I refer to when I approach the topic with students, some of whom are unfamiliar with the term 'second person' but understand and have employed first and third person perspective in their writing practice. Contrary to conventional theory, second person is not a point of view, but a form of address, so every second person address also has a first or third person narration running alongside it. Once student writers understand that difference, they are able to experiment with second person to write stories that differ from 'traditional' storytelling to produce interesting – sometimes stunning – effects.

Perhaps the most natural way into using the second person in prose is to start with the epistolary. Most students write letters, or at least emails, from time to time.

The exercise
Prompt students to:
1. write a letter to their twelve-year-old self. The tone can be one of congratulation or warning or a combination of both;
2. write a letter from one fictional character to another. They have had a big disagreement. Use the letter to advance or justify the argument.

After students have tried one or both of these exercises, ask them to drop the salutations and addressee's details and see if the piece works without identifying that it's a letter. Then ask them to rewrite and edit until it becomes a story that climaxes with an epiphany or turning point.

The objective
By writing a letter addressed to themselves or to a fictional character, the student can set a tone of self-examination, even self-condemnation, that adds an interesting slant to a story. The use of the second person can have the effect of involving the reader in the story. Although the story might be very personal to the writer or character, it can add a universal aspect so that readers can identify closely with the protagonist, drawing them in. At the same time, the second-person address can also add distance in a way that a first-person monologue doesn't. Sometimes this frees students to write creative non-fiction that they feel comfortable sharing.

Another approach: how-to stories
Once students have explored the epistolary form, you might want to try other ways of using the second person

form of address. The instructional or 'how-to' form is another interesting and fun way in.

The exercise
Prepare postcards by writing the following lines on each:
• How to build a home
• How to leave a country
• How to tame a lion
• How to become a writer
• How to throw a party
• How to spend your money
• How to spoil a weekend
• How to talk to your father.

Ask your students to choose one and start free writing for five minutes. If they like they can start by making a list. If they do choose to make a list, point out that each item on the list can be expanded, explored and explained. Once links are made, a story will start to appear. I encourage students to write in their own time then bring the story to the workshop and rewrite in response to the workshop comments and suggestions.

The objective
These 'how-to' stories are not conventional. Time does not work in the same way as in a traditional story. While the instruction is in the future tense, the story that emerges will be in the past tense. The instruction is given to the second person (the 'you' is either stated or supposed) by a first-person narrator who is almost invisible. These factors can produce a unique tone that becomes the focus of the story.

Contributor: Barrie Llewelyn

Because Barrie is an unusual name for a girl, when asked about it I sometimes say that Barrie comes from the Assyrian and means my parents wanted a boy. In reality, I was named after a dancer called Barrie Chase who, my mother insists, was Fred Astaire's favourite dance partner. I write fiction, non-fiction and poetry. Sometimes, I work as an editor. I recommend *Bird by bird* by Anne Lamott. Ask me if you need to know the causes of the American Civil War, but I can't help you with plumbing or trainspotting. If I didn't tell you, you'd never know that I have a secret crush on entrepreneur and TV personality, Lord Alan Sugar.

24

The paperless workshop: save trees, increase interaction, reduce preciousness

Introduction
The workshop is the standard model for the teaching of creative writing at all levels. Workshopping uses a lot of paper, printing and photocopying multiple copies of student work, which is then usually annotated by peers and tutors. While this method may be useful for students with manuscripts at a late stage of development, when work is further from completion, it is not as helpful as it might be. The very act of printing off gives a spurious sense of completion, rendering students unwilling to do more than change the odd word or phrase and reluctant to look at larger issues of structure and shape.

Conventional paper-based workshopping in creative writing also operates on a limited model of serial 'spokes of the wheel' interaction: one after another each person has their say, thus giving an artificial hierarchy of opinion, and putting artificial pressures on each subsequent contributor to come up with something original.

In contrast, on-screen and on-line workshopping encourage a more flexible and interactive paradigm, where all participants can share thoughts and suggestions that can be seen and evaluated immediately. This enriches and expands the learning experience as all students gain an immediate insight into the complex and ever-shifting writer/reader relationship absent from, or obscured in, paper-based workshops.

Preparation

Ideally each member of the workshop will have a computer with internet access, and this is the starting point I will assume, though there are various possibilities with shared use of computers, or even with only one computer with screen projection, where as lecturer you can demonstrate exemplary editing techniques.

Students with writing to workshop should have it in electronic form, either on a memory stick or via email. There's no need to circulate the work beforehand. You then need to access a document sharing site and invite the group to view the shared material. Currently, I use sites based on the now discontinued EtherPad technologies, such as PiratePad (http://piratepad.net) or Typewithme (http://typewith.me). These sites have the advantage of being free, and requiring no log-in or passwords. However, new technologies are emerging all the time, so by the time you read this there may be other possibilities.

Now, technology and hardware willing, you and your whole group should be looking at the same document. All of you have equal, synchronous and virtually instantaneous ability to edit the main document. For students, this situation usually proves interesting if not exciting. It also demands certain protocols of respect and trust.

The exercises

For a lecturer, simultaneous access to a document gives an enormous variety of workshopping possibilities, among which are:

1. Get a student to paste an extract of their work into the shared document. Then, conduct a masterclass-style

editing demonstration, cutting, pasting, moving, rearranging. You can demonstrate changes of register and tone, show how altering order of events changes the way a story impacts on readers, and, of course, point out any changes in point of view.

Now invite members of the group to do the editing, either singly, or in pairs. Invite strategic comments and questions: so rather than 'Why have you used "sofa" and not "settee"?' maybe, 'Why have you set this scene in the parlour?' or, 'Do you need this scene at all? What purpose does it serve?'

The next step is to edit the work as a group, discussing choices and decisions, then get someone to read the piece out loud, and ask the group to highlight the parts that bring images alive in their heads.

2. Create a wholly new collaborative piece of work starting from nothing. This works particularly well for script. For example, pick a well-known story (e.g. a fairy tale), and then get the group to write it down in its key elements. Everyone can chip in at once. From the resultant energetic mess, work towards an agreed structure. Discuss where to start and where to finish, decide on scenes and their order, and then get people to write the scenes singly or in small groups. Then 'perform' the entire script.

3. Select a famous writer whose unedited work has been subsequently published. Paste in an extract from the unedited text. Get the group to edit it down, and then reveal the 'right answer' in terms of final published text.

It's worth noting that in none of these cases does the electronic interaction necessarily replace face-to-face interaction; rather, it supplements and enhances it. However, this kind of technology obviously opens up possibilities for international collaborations and remote workshopping.

Students whose work has been looked at have something useful to take away with them that is much easier to access and ponder than multiple marked-up paper copies. Not only can they save the final edited draft complete with suggestions and comments, but many of these document sharing sites have a 'time slider' facility that makes it possible to see the whole editing process replayed, including false starts and rejected changes. And of course, as lecturer, you can use the same facility to check who has contributed, and who hasn't.

The objective

These exercises are based on a Discipline-focused Learning Technology Enhancement Academy project supported by the UK's Higher Education Academy. The objective was to get students to look at their writing in a less precious and more flexible way. In addition, they learn a wide range of editing strategies and techniques and save whole forests of trees.

Contributor: Steve May

My name is Steve May, but I sometimes use other names to avoid litigation. I write plays, books and the occasional poem, and I recommend that you read *Doing creative writing* (by Steve May). Ask me if you need information on Alekhine's defence; I can't build a dagoba. You'd never have known if I hadn't told you that we went to the same school, but never met.

25

Put it on a postcard: capturing the poetic moment in prose

Introduction
This exercise works in a number of contexts equally well, and with any level of student. Originally conceived of as a way into thinking about writing prose poems, over time I've found that students responding with the full range of creative writing genres – fiction, verse poetry, and memoir – also find the exercise useful and stretching. It naturally highlights tensions and sympathies between the narrative impulse and the poetic one, encouraging compression and metaphor as ways of reaching for 'the poetic moment' in the ordinary.

The exercise
I circulate plain white postcards of the type sold in leaved packs in stationery shops. In these, one whole face is entirely blank; this is the writing surface.

I ask students to recall something striking from the previous two days: something they have witnessed, participated in, observed, heard about, etc., or that simply struck them as being important or resonant. Occasionally an inexperienced group may find this first step a hurdle, in which case five minutes of individual brainstorming helps focus recall and observations. From the brainstormed list a moment or event that feels important can then be chosen.

Whichever way the moment or event is arrived at, the exercise works best if the moment's potential meaning is not yet fully realised or known. What's important is the sense that 'something is going on here', so I encourage students to follow their gut feeling.

Students then have fifteen minutes to capture their moment or event on a single postcard in *prose form*. I encourage them to use all the conventions of prose they need: e.g. dialogue, time markers, gesture, and character. They may re-draft the piece onto another postcard if they wish; this often happens as students refine their editing in order to fit the event to the space available.

After fifteen minutes, I invite them to share their work and, as a group, discuss the choices they had to make in tackling the exercise. Issues that usually arise are dealing with starting points, endings, and feeling the need to understand the meaning or 'poetry' of the moment before being able to complete the task. Issues around the use of language, prose rhythm versus poetic line or rhythm, and 'how much story' to include, also tend to emerge.

The objective

The exercise has self-evident applications for the making of prose poems. It immediately highlights tensions between poetry and prose: students look for a 'moment', but write a 'story' about it. The confined space requires them to grapple with economy of language, and to address directly time, pace and expression. In doing so, both poets and prose writers often find that they have produced interestingly distilled work, privileging aspects of it in unaccustomed but potentially rich ways. They usually find too that their work has been placed under an unusual tension, one at the centre of prose poetry. For some students, this is enough for them to set off in the exploration of an unfamiliar but intriguing new form.

In other contexts – fiction, poetry, memoir, craft and technique classes – this exercise encourages the examination of how meaning is captured on the page. It emphasises economy in all forms, and illustrates how constraint can stimulate invention, and how the resulting tension can result in real impact. This might be a resonant moment in prose, a transcendent moment in poetry, a moment beyond anecdote in memoir. On a practical level, the exercise hones students' writing skills by encouraging close editing and the development of sophisticated control in order to achieve clarity and precision.

Most broadly, this exercise develops critical awareness and a writerly observation of the everyday, practices at the heart of almost all forms of creative writing.

Contributor: Patricia Debney
I was due to be born on St Patrick's Day, a big deal in the States. In the event I was five days late, but my parents hung onto the name. I write prose poems, memoir, and fiction. I keep a blog: www.wavingdrowning.wordpress.com. Ask me if you need information about coastal terminology or children with Type 1 diabetes. I can't help you with electricity. You'd never know unless I told you that I grew up in the Blue Ridge Mountains of Virginia.

26

Finding a suitable narrative voice when writing for children

Introduction
Writing for children is a very specialised activity. Jean Piaget tells us that children go through different stages in a set order (Elkind, *Children and adolescents, interpretive essays on Piaget*). Whilst these stages happen at different ages for individual children, and each stage lasts a different length of time for each child, the stages always follow in the same order and none are missed out. Laura Berk (*Child development*) has expanded on Piaget's work and offers us details about what happens at each stage of development. Those of us who wish to write for children would do well to use the work of Berk and Piaget, alongside the intuition arising from our own childhood memories.

The exercise
The narrative voice comes out of the gap between the writer and the notional reader. First then, we need to establish who these two people are.

Begin by asking the students to remember a pleasant scene from their own childhood. Then ask them to write that scene for about twenty minutes, as if they are speaking to their own younger selves. It is quite interesting to use second person for this. This helps them to remember what it was like being a child.

Next ask them to imagine the child who will read their story by answering the character questionnaire below. When they have done that, do the same exercise for the narrator of their story. The questions are just suggestions; you may alter them as you wish, but they should certainly deal with physical, intellectual and emotional detail as well as personality traits and what is important to their target reader and to the narrator.

CHARACTER QUESTIONNAIRE
What do they look like?
How old are they?
How used are they to their own height and strength?
What would they like to eat?
How are they doing at school? What are they good at, what are they bad at?
How do they get on with authority figures?
What sort of job would they like?
What do they most like to do in their free time?
What sort of stories do they like?
What might be their favourite type of TV programme?
What do they worry about most?
Who are they getting on well with?
From whom do they feel peer pressure?
Are there other adults in their lives apart from their parents?
What makes them happy?
What makes them sad?
What makes them angry?
Which quality do they admire most in others?
What are they most afraid of?
What is their greatest wish?

Allow your students to spend quite a bit of time on this. You could allow twenty minutes in class and also set it as homework. They don't need to write a lot but they do need to devote considerable thought to the character of the narrator and notional reader before they start work on the story.

Incidentally, these questions are also useful for creating characters within the story. If the exercise is spread between two classes, it is likely that your students will begin to find a story.

Now they should rewrite the memory scene they thought of earlier, or they may write a scene from a story they have in mind or from a story that has suggested itself as they did this exercise. This time they should try out the narrative voice they think would suit their story – in any tense or person that feels right, such as first person present tense or third person past tense, being careful all the time to remember the reader they have imagined. Allow twenty minutes.

Often at this point the students surprise themselves by finding the narrator and imagined reader are different ages from each other and/or from the age of the child they thought they wanted to write for. It is in fact quite common for children to want to read about characters two years older than themselves. Often the narrator will emerge as a child about two years older than the reader. Sometimes, though, the narrative voice will resemble an older sibling, aunt or uncle or even a grandparent.

Ask them then to experiment with changing the person and/or the tense – reading the piece aloud will help the writer to gauge which person/tense combination works best. Encourage them to try several combinations on a

112

pivotal part of the text. Ideally this is done as homework and brought to the following class. Note that using second person can give a very fresh and unusual voice, though it is hard to sustain. The first person often works very well in texts written for older children as it can encourage intimacy and in some cases help the reader to grow with the narrator.

The use of the present tense brings some immediacy, though care must be taken that it doesn't sound as though the narrator is walking around notebook in hand.

The objective

This exercise helps to focus students' attention on the importance of perceiving both the narrator and the reader to be additional characters in the telling of the story. A gap between the time the idea is first presented to students and when they have to produce a text allows them to get to know these two important additional characters really well.

There is often a concern in writers that they have not found their voice, nor ever will. Yet different texts need different voices and this exercise brings an honesty and ease to finding the voice that suits a particular story. Certainly, if students want to write for a variety of ages they'll need a variety of voices. They may also discover which age group they prefer to write for and start to appreciate the difference between the writer and the writing persona involved in establishing narrative voice.

The 'patch test' of trying different tenses and persons encourages reading text out loud, an activity that can also be used later as part of other editing processes. The students sharpen their instincts and increase their confidence in those instincts, as they begin to recognise which combination sounds and feels right.

Contributor: Gill James

My name is Gill James. If I had been a boy, I would have been Gilbert, named after the grandfather I never met. I live in Manchester. I write fiction and educational materials for children and young adults, and some short fiction for adults. I have recently developed an interest in science fiction. See www.gilljames.co.uk and http://www.seek.salford.ac.uk/profiles/GJAMES.jsp. I recommend that you read *Write for children* by Andrew Melrose. When I'm not writing, I like to go for walks in the countryside. Ask me if you need information about French, German or Spanish. I can't help you with accounting or football. If I didn't tell you, you'd never know that I sing the tenor part in a choir.

27

Writing with Shakespeare and Montaigne: past practices for future writers

Introduction

'And what are these things I scribble,' writes Montaigne, 'other than grotesques and monstrous bodies, patched together without any order, connection, or proportion except what's accidental?' (*Les essais*, vol. 1, p.105; my translation).

Montaigne describes his work in a way that's quite alien from our usual expectations of carefully crafted student work. Imagine assigning students to write with no order, connection, or proportion? Yet that's what I'm going to suggest you do. This exercise guides students through the process used by Montaigne. It also exemplifies a general pedagogical approach: teach not only the work of historical writers, but also the historical writing practices used to create them. Students may have read 'On friendship' or *Romeo and Juliet*, but seldom do they know how Shakespeare or Montaigne worked. In these exercises, they get to find out and, better yet, try out their writing practices for themselves.

Exercise 1: Montaigne and commonplaces

I give students copies of these extracts from Cicero's 'On divination', as quoted by Montaigne (*Les essais*, vol. 2, p. 471; my translation):

> What he sees often, he doesn't wonder at, although he doesn't know how it happened. Yet when a thing happens that he's never seen, he thinks it's a portentous wonder.
>
> Only once things have passed can some interpretation find them to have been prophesised.

I then ask them to write a very short personal essay with the working title, 'On a monstrous child'. They are free to interpret the title in any manner they wish, but they must incorporate the two quotations into the body of their essay.

After fifteen to twenty minutes, I stop them and do a brief presentation on the Renaissance practice of keeping a commonplace book and how authors used these 'commonplaces' – pithy or profound quotations from classical authors such as Cicero, Ovid, and Virgil, usually organised around particular topics – to create their work.

As an example, I distribute copies of Montaigne's 'On a monstrous child', in which he uses the quotations from Cicero, and read it aloud. When we reach those quotations, students usually release a collective ah-ha: they suddenly see that they've written with the same commonplaces as Montaigne and in a like manner. We then read aloud a few of their essays to see how the same commonplaces lead to vastly different essays.

The exercise closes with our collective exploration of the Montaigne quote I used to open: how is writing like a 'monstrous body' and how are commonplaces like the limbs and organs from which monsters get made? How might we use this practice in our own writing?

Exercise 2: Shakespeare and source use
I give students two excerpts from different versions of the

Romeo and Juliet story. Both capture the moment when Romeo first sees Juliet.

FROM ARTHUR BROOKE'S *The tragicall historye of Romeus and Iuliet* (1562)

>   With upright beam he weighed
>   the beauty of each dame,
>   And judged who best and who next her
>   was wrought in nature's frame.
>   At length he saw a maid,
>   right fair of perfect shape,
>   Which Theseus or Paris would
>   have chosen to their rape,
>   Whom erst he ever saw,
>   of all she pleased him most.
>   Within himself he said to her,
>   "Thou justly may thee boast
>   Of perfect shape's renown
>   and Beauty's sounding praise,
>   Whose like nay has, nay shall be seen,
>   nay liveth in our days."

FROM WILLIAM SHAKESPEARE'S *Tragedie of Romeo and Juliet* (1597)

>   O, she doth teach the torches to burn bright!
>   It seems she hangs upon the cheek of night
>   As a rich jewel in an Ethiop's ear –
>   Beauty too rich for use, for earth too dear!
>   So shows a snowy dove trooping with crows
>   As yonder lady o'er her fellows shows.
>   The measure done, I'll watch her place of stand,
>   And, touching hers, make blessèd my rude hand.
>   Did my heart love till now? Forswear it, sight!
>   For I ne'er saw true beauty till this night.

Slowly, the realisation that Shakespeare composed his most famous tragedy from another book dawns on students. I inform them that pillaging sources was a common practice among Renaissance writers. Moreover, to write *Romeo and Juliet*, Shakespeare borrowed not only from Brooke's poem, but several other works. The story of these star-crossed lovers goes back in Italy to at least 1476.

This context allows us to achieve our first aim: figure out why Shakespeare's version of the story became famous. We do so by comparing the two excerpts and teasing out Shakespeare's technique: his use of imagery, emotion, and the poetic line. Pinpointing these techniques sets up students for our second aim: adapt those techniques to write a contemporary version of the same scene.

For the next ten minutes, the students use both Brooke's poem and Shakespeare's play as sources to create their scenes, which they can do in either prose or verse and which usually end up ranging from farce to tragedy. And, as they read them aloud, they hear themselves participating in a storytelling tradition and a writing practice that starts before Shakespeare, continues for over 400 years, and now includes them.

The objective

The primary goal of these exercises is to expand, historically and practically, how students go about writing their work. They also alert students to the ways in which writers use the work of writers who precede them.

But writing with Montaigne and Shakespeare can be inspiring too. Suddenly these immortal works no longer appear as always-existing monuments of literature that dropped from the heavens. Instead, students see them as the result of specific writing practices, practices they can use and adapt to their own ends.

Contributor: Eric LeMay

My full name is Eric Charles LeMay. My middle name comes from my grandfather. I live in Athens, Ohio, a small town in the foothills of the Appalachian mountain range. I write non-fiction and poetry. You can find it at http://www.ericlemay.org. I recommend *Crafting the personal essay: a guide for writing and publishing Creative Non-Fiction* by Dinty W. Moore. Ask me if you need information on cheese – I wrote a book about it. If I didn't tell you, you'd never know that I'm beginning to prefer the leaves on trees to those in books.

28

Earth, Air, Fire and Water:
a writing and performance workshop

Introduction

Most of us are aware that the weather affects our moods but harnessing the dramatic potential of the four elements can help energise writing by even the most experienced of practitioners. The interaction between humans and nature will always be central to our lives and the four elements have provided inspiration for writers and artists since the beginning of recorded time.

This exercise is one I devised to get undergraduate students to write and perform as a team but I have also used it successfully with professional writers. It is particularly effective in helping to establish a healthy group dynamic for newly formed classes. Writing in the voice of one of the elements can help to get students' writing to flow and performing as a team boosts their confidence.

The exercise

SETTING IT UP

I usually introduce the workshop by getting students to think of any novels, poems or plays in which the elements act as a catalyst for change or particularly influence the lives of the protagonists. Suggestions usually range from popular ones like *Wuthering Heights* by Emily Brontë or *Mill on the Floss* by George Eliot, to *Drought* by J.G. Ballard. Some discussion of these examples might follow.

As additional stimulation, sound tracks of water, air, and fire can be downloaded from various internet sites.

You will need a number of large pieces of paper, or rolls of plain wallpaper, and enough coloured pens to be distributed amongst the groups.

STAGE 1

Each student is assigned one of the four elements: earth, air, fire and water. They are asked to write a list of any associations they make with their assigned element, whether it is one of its properties or an image or a verb of motion. I allow a few minutes only for this warm-up.

STAGE 2

Students write in the voice of their element, describing what happens when Fire meets Water or when Air meets Earth. A few minutes ought to be enough for this exercise too.

STAGE 3

Next they are asked to use some of the words from their list to write an extended sentence in which they write in the voice of their element, describing one of the effects this force can have (e.g. 'I am Air that blows the north wind down the valley in violent blusters that whip round the house and shake the shutters').

PERFORMANCE

Students are all asked to stand up and read out their pieces simultaneously as loudly as they can, competing with one another's voices and being as dramatic or as restrained as they wish to be. They might read out in groups of any combination of the elements: all the Water voices, all the

121

Air voices, and so forth. They are often quite reluctant to do this first reading so applause is essential. With a very shy group, the lecturer taking part can help get them going. Most students are suitably exhilarated and warmed up after this first plunge and ready for the collaboration.

Some discussion is necessary at this stage to widen associations and discover where students' imaginations are transporting them.

COLLABORATIVE WRITING AND PERFORMANCE

Form the students into groups of four consisting of a representative of each of the elements. If students wish to swap elements with another student, they may do so at this stage. They will now work together to produce a poem or choral piece writing in the voice of the elements so it's useful to offer some advice on collaboration. This may include the following:

They need to decide on the focus and performance plan.

Are they each going to work on their own piece or are they going to arrange it as choral voices that address and respond to one another, as in an opera?

Are they going to write their own lines of poetry that are then joined together by a refrain or a chorus?

Each group then has fifteen to twenty minutes to write and prepare their collaborative piece for performance.

At least ten minutes needs to be scheduled for each group to perform and discuss their writing with the rest of the students as audience.

The objective

Simulating the motion of the elements and exploring associations loosens the pen and encourages free thinking, as students have the freedom to take their focus in any direction they please. It unfailingly leads to interesting and fluid writing and might be useful near the beginning of a course of say, ten workshops, as the benefits can be enjoyed for longer. Students often report an increase in confidence and courage, in that they feel able to tackle themes they might not have contemplated before. The collaboration established in this workshop could be extended to a number of sessions in which participants develop an extended piece of performance poetry.

For the lecturer, these exercises offer an opportunity to observe students interacting and see how the small groups gel. It is surprisingly uplifting to hear the voices of the other workshop participants and can be enormously helpful in establishing a trusting workshop in which students feel confident about reading their work and voicing their opinions.

Contributor: Lisa Samson

My name is Lisa Samson. I was given my Christian name because a woman in the village was going to call her baby Lisa, but she had a boy so my mother took the name for me. I live in North Yorkshire and I write fiction and non-fiction in which landscape figures prominently. I recommend *Poetry in the making* by Ted Hughes. Ask me if you need information on cooking Italian food or hiking in Yorkshire. I can't help you with physics or gardening. If I didn't tell you, you'd never know that I speak fluent Italian.

29

Gift wraps: a collaborative poetry game

Introduction
This exercise offers itself for playing with different levels of sophistication by adults or children, down to the youngest age at which participants can write down their own ideas. Physically handing the written words over is part of the game. It offers a rapid and unthreatening way into fresh ideas for less confident writers while inviting subtle responses from experienced writers and participants already part of a creative writing culture. The interaction is between two people, so this can be done in groups of any size. The outcome for each pair is a short poem, easy to share with a larger group. The ethos is that the resulting pieces become something more than either individual had imagined. The participants feel ownership but the poem acquires a life of its own.

The only resources needed are something to write with and loose sheets of paper that can be passed on. The writing time can be as little as fifteen minutes; the time taken to lead into it, with examples, is variable, as is the time to share it at the end.

The exercise
TALKING US INTO THE ZONE
As in most writing exercises, the lecturer's job is to create an ambience – in this case, to remind participants of an impulse that is almost universal. The idea of a poem as a

gift – for a loved one, for a birthday – is part of our popular culture: look at birthday cards and Valentines in any card shop. It is also deep in the history of poetry, and can convey complicated feelings. Edward Thomas's 'And you, Helen' (*Collected poems*) or Carol Ann Duffy's 'Valentine' (*Mean time*) are examples I often use to illustrate this to a student group.

I find it useful to discuss the nature of surprises – not everyone enjoys them and some are unwelcome, but the unexpected is what gives life to a poem. In this exercise they can create small wonders and surprises, with the help of their group.

All collaboration is a trust game. As lecturer, it's vital to sponsor a sense of playfulness that also acknowledges that genuine feelings might also be at stake. The metaphor of child-rearing comes naturally: each participant is letting some of their ideas 'leave home'; the pleasure is seeing what they might grow into.

Writing

Ask each student to think of a real person who inspires a strong feeling – good, bad or complicated. This game is best of all for complicated feelings that are hard to put into words so it's important to point out that nobody will be asked to name the person they are thinking of or the reason for their feelings. I am usually upfront in saying that this is only a starting point; the poem sets out from here but might well undergo a change.

Offer the idea of a poem as an opportunity to give this person an impossible gift, something only words can conjure, then ask the students to do the following, working in pairs:

Write a single word or phrase, starting with
I want to give you...
e.g. *...the earth*
...a portable hole

Now pass the paper on to their partner. Do not talk about it at this stage.

When they receive their partner's line, their job is to flesh the idea out, to make it more remarkable, but adding an unexpected detail in a second line.

e.g. *... the earth*
tied up in a big pink ribbon

... a portable hole
so you can escape whenever you feel trapped

Now they should swap papers again, without any discussion. The element of surprise, of not knowing where this is leading, is part of the pleasure.

The next stage, once each student has received back the sheet they started with, is to add two or three lines to clinch it. At this point, remind the students of how many ways there are for a poem to reach closure – with a punch line, a joke, a twist or an open-ended haunting image.

e.g. *... the earth*
tied up in a big pink ribbon
like red sky in the morning, shepherd's warning –
there'll be thunderstorms to come

... a portable hole
so you can escape whenever you feel trapped
like you say you do with me.
OK, have it your own way –
here, catch!

Sharing
This depends on size of group and time and situation. Poems can be read out by their originating writers to the whole group, acknowledging their partners, or posted on a notice board to read. They can also be shared in small groups, who select one that they feel contains, and yet makes fit, the greatest surprise. Read these back to the whole group, maybe anonymously: the poems read out are not 'winners' but represent the shared discernment of the group.

The objective
This exercise can build trust in a group, especially one newly constituted. Partners in the game will often enjoy observing *how* they played it with each other – e.g. by going along with the mood suggested by the given lines, or by subverting/teasing them, or offering a challenge; by leaning towards everyday realism, or fantasy.

It can also produce a first piece of writing in a writing class/day/weekend, overcoming 'starter's block'.

Finally, it can raise through practice some fundamental thoughts about poetry:

a) a poem may evolve in ways the writers did not originally intend and yet which satisfies and pleases them in the end;

b) an unexpected input or chance find can stimulate the writer's imagination in response;

c) the power and originality of a poem often lies in its ability to link apparently disparate elements into an organic-feeling whole.

Whether we like it or not, every poem we write 'leaves home' and is open to creative re-interpretation by its readers; this game shows students that process in action and, because the writer can respond in turn, it can be experienced not as loss of control but as a creative opportunity.

Contributor: Philip Gross

Philip Gross has a surname that hints at the ebb and flow of occupations, wars and displacements in his father's homeland, Estonia. Poetry is his heartland, feeding into novels for young people and into drama of several kinds; see www.philipgross.co.uk. He recommends Celia Hunt and Fiona Sampson's *Writing, self and reflexivity*. Ask him about selkies or coelacanths, not about celebs. And if you wonder why he is writing about himself in the third person, it's because he thinks stepping a little outside himself, as on a mountain top or in a Quaker meeting, makes him more, not less, himself.

30

Write what you know:
fictionalising every day experience

Introduction
One of the most important and often cited means through which writers create fiction is by drawing on their own experiences, observations and views of the world. While the premise 'write what you know' seems simple enough, how it's done can be challenging. For new writers especially, drawing on their own wells of experience and then developing fragments of observation into creative work is not always a readily or comfortably adopted practice. While this exercise exploits some of the processes connected with autobiographical writing, it should also enable students to start producing work that develops more clearly within the realms of fiction.

This exercise first of all illustrates how our memory and our own lens of perception can be used as a way of creating material that is enhanced through our creative and literary imagination. In addition to this, the exercise demonstrates the need for writers to be attentive to detail and to record and later use data in their creative writing.

The exercise
This exercise works well over two taught face-to-face sessions, but the instructions to students below can be easily adapted and used, for example, through online instructions/teaching.

STAGE 1

Ask your students to close their eyes and to try and recall their journey here today from the moment they set off. Ask them to think about the route they took, the people they saw or interacted with on the way, the mode/s of transport used, any street signs or furniture that they thought interesting. In short, ask them to recall anything they noticed or found memorable. These recollections do not have to be particularly remarkable, unusual or different; even the mundane, trivial and ordinary elements of the journey should be kept in mind.

STAGE 2

As soon as they think they have enough material, they can open their eyes and write down those details that they can remember. At this point, they should be writing quickly and in note, list or 'trigger word' form.

STAGE 3

Once they have made these notes, ask them to work them into a piece of autobiographical writing where they explore the physical and mental aspects of the journey. The first person is an obvious and effective point of view to use for this part of the exercise.

When conducting the exercise over two face-to-face sessions, the first one would end here with Stage 4 given as homework.

STAGE 4

The next time they make the same journey, they should do their best to make/take notes in real time. This is obviously easier for students taking the bus or train, but if they happen to be driving or on foot, they can make notes when it is safe to do so. They may find a voice recorder useful.

STAGE 5

At the next face-to-face meeting, in order to produce a more detailed segment of writing, ask the students to combine the material they produced at stage 3 with the new research notes they completed in stage 4.

As well as adding a further layer of depth and texture, at this stage they should be encouraged to allow their imagination to exert some influence on the writing. By having this piece of largely autobiographical writing as a new starting point, they also have the capacity to deviate from what they actually saw, felt and experienced.

How they do this is largely up to them but they can, for example, exploit overheard conversations, imagine and construct realities, identities and thoughts of the strangers they saw or interacted with.

To round off the exercise, it's interesting to ask students to explore and then discuss the specifics of their work; in particular the extent to which the pieces of writing changed after the research stage. They can also be invited to read segments of their work from across the drafting/ research/writing stages and, finally, encouraged to spend some time writing a brief reflective piece about the process more generally.

Variations
By repeating this exercise using different settings or contexts, students should be able to enhance their capacity to use their own perception as a starting point for creating

materials that can be developed into well formed writing. For example, students don't have to rely on the recollection of journeys. Instead, you can ask them to recall events and moments which have occurred in different places and times: a classroom at school; some of the people they know at work; their feelings when they hear a particular song or watch a certain film. In short, by recalling memories and then adding a further layer of research, students are in the process of constructing a foundation their creativity and imagination can build upon.

The objective

The overarching aim of this exercise is to demonstrate how real life situations can become contexts and settings in which imagination is given literary license and freedom. In order to exercise the imagination, it's necessary to give it scope and opportunity to roam and flourish. Through embracing real life as a means of producing writing, students can further enhance their style, voice and control.

Contributor: M.Y. Alam

My name is M.Y. Alam. I write novels and short stories (see http://www.route-online.com/authors/m-y-alam.html). I'm also a social researcher working in the areas of social cohesion, ethnic relations and mass media. I recommend you read Stephen King's *On writing: a memoir of the craft*. When I'm not writing, I enjoy watching movies and reading, as well as playing sports, especially badminton and football. Ask me if you need information on popular culture or identity politics. I can't help you with hair care products. You'd never have known if I hadn't told you that I used to manage a snooker club.

31

Structuring the perfect short story: how to create a strong plot arc

Introduction
I always think of short stories as having more in common with poems than novels as they should be a complete experience, focusing on one main issue. I've found over the years that one thing that marks out an excellent short story from a mediocre one is a tight structure with a strong dramatic arc that leads the reader through the main character's experience in a complete and satisfying way.

It is also important to understand that in most adult genres physical action is not enough to create this arc. A soldier being asked to shoot someone then doing so is not enough of an arc by itself. A soldier being terrified of firing a gun because he saw his father being shot when he was young, and overcoming this to do the task required of him in a war situation is.

The exercise
This exercise is designed to help writers plot out the perfect short story by opening with one key issue, building it to a crisis point and then resolving it.

STARTING THE EXERCISE – PREPARATORY WORK
Ask your students to think up a basic idea for a story or, if they wish, to recall the idea at the heart of a story they have written but do not feel satisfied with. This works equally

well online or face to face. You should then ask them to complete three simple processes – you can choose whether to issue the instructions separately or in a batch, perhaps as a handout:

1. Write down in one sentence what their story is about. For example, 'Jacqui is sixteen and feels she should be allowed way more independence than her overprotective mother is giving her.'
2. From that sentence, they should clarify exactly what emotional issue their story is addressing. In the example, it is resentment of imposed rules.
3. Their next task is to decide what viewpoint they are going to write the story from and make sure it's the one which can best illustrate the journey in the story.

Using the example, it should be Jacqui's viewpoint as she is the one feeling the resentment and it would be a very passive tale from the mother's viewpoint.

THE MAIN EXERCISE

Now, ask your students to plot out their story arc, pinpointing the three key areas discussed above:

1. Where their story starts: this should be the point at which the emotional issue really begins to come to a head.
2. How the story builds to a crisis point: this will form the central part of their story and it is vital that they know exactly where they are going to keep their narrative tight and pacey and to draw the reader through.
3. How the issue is resolved: they don't have to have a happy ending, or necessarily to tie up all the threads, but they do need the main character to move on in the course of the story or what's the point in a reader spending their valuable time reading about them?

You may find it useful to provide a table for students to fill in for clarity, as shown here using my example:

WHERE THE STORY STARTS
It could be just as Jacqui heads out to a party saying her older boyfriend will bring her back at one a.m., a time her mother is not happy with at all. Jacqui is furious at this lack of trust.

HOW THE STORY BUILDS TO A CRISIS POINT
Jacqui, having compromised on midnight, is persuaded by her boyfriend to rebel and stay an extra hour, but she then finds that he still doesn't want to leave. The party is getting rowdy and she's frightened and wants to go home but can't control the situation. She wants her mum!

HOW THE ISSUE IS RESOLVED
Jacqui rings her mum who rushes out to rescue her and, far from being judgemental, is very understanding. They agree to work together on letting her grow up gradually. The rules will still be there, but Jacqui no longer resents them.

The objective
The students should end up with the structural basis of a strong short story. They must be encouraged to make sure that the issue is an emotional one, in which something changes for their character. It is also vital that the issue remains the same throughout and does not drift to a slightly different one. In my example, this could be that Jacqui decides she hates her boyfriend – this may happen in the course of the story but cannot be its core resolution. Once this structural spine is in place, they can go on to write the whole story.

Contributor: Joanna Barnden

My name is Joanna Barnden but I'm Jo to friends or Oj to my Dad. I write short stories, serials and novels – www. joannabarnden.co.uk. When not writing, I like to read when the kids let me, walk the dog when the kids will leave the house, or travel – once the kids have left home! Ask me if you need any information on women's magazines but I can't help you with directions to anywhere. If I didn't tell you, you'd never have known that I have two rowing gold medals from Henley Regatta.

32

Hands-on activities for experimental drama: crafting and directing spectacles

Introduction

Most students have been exposed to countless television sitcoms and Hollywood blockbusters, but relatively few plays. Even if one is gifted with students who are avid theatregoers, it's likely they'll have attended mostly mainstream musicals, Shakespeare productions, and realistic drama in the vein of Arthur Miller or Neil Simon. When students write plays, they unconsciously follow the dramaturgical conventions of familiar models. Helping students become aware of the wide array of theatrical traditions and possibilities of the stage is essential if they are to make use of dramatic conventions rather than be used by them. A playwriting lecturer can help students recognise a variety of theatrical traditions by critically examining the historical contexts that gave rise to different dramaturgical conventions, incorporating hands-on activities that utilise unfamiliar theatre traditions, and allowing students to direct productions of short experimental plays as well as their classmates' scripts.

The exercise

The playwriting lecturer cannot simply be content with reading and analysing written texts as models. The power of lesser-known theatrical traditions such as opera, mime, improvisation, masques, puppetry, and *commedia dell'arte* – as well as non-Western forms of theatre such as Kabuki,

137

Noh, Balinese shadow-play, or Sanskrit drama – cannot be conveyed through scripts alone. These traditions require an understanding of body language, gesture, ritual, slapstick, music, comic timing, masks, puppets, and costumes; knowledge that is crucial for any developing playwright. When introducing these forms of drama, even brief video clips of performances will make a profound impact on students' comprehension. Since foreign modes of drama upset many standard assumptions that beginning playwrights have about the theatre, situating any tradition in its historical context and discussing the cultural forces that motivated its models of performance will offer a fuller appreciation for its unique form.

To help students understand new theatrical forms and challenge their received notions of theatre, engage students in hands-on activities that make use of spectacle. Before any writing is done on paper, have students improvise characters, create masks and puppets, choreograph a dance, design a slapstick routine, or compose a song. Select the activity that parallels the theatrical tradition you have chosen to investigate, since students benefit from depth rather than breadth of exposure to unfamiliar types of drama.

Rather than beginning with dialogue, I assign students to write a script that takes its starting-point from one or more of the materials they have created. Building texts around spectacle will allow more dynamic scripts, which can be further encouraged by offering opportunities to stage the text after its completion.

Staging scripts

Allowing students to direct short experimental plays in the classroom will give them insight into how drama is constructed. Many students who are initially averse to avant-garde theatre will eventually want to appropriate some of its styles and techniques once they experience directing a production. I have found that allowing students to direct micro-plays of a page or two by Samuel Beckett (*Collected shorter plays*) or Suzan-Lori Parks (*365 days/365 plays*), for example, helps them understand the way that words connect to theatrical concepts like set, body movement, and costume. While you can't always take students to the theatre, you can bring theatre into the classroom.

Students who perform and direct, rather than simply read texts, will learn the varieties of ways that the page relates to the stage, which is especially important in construing the significance of experimental plays. With smaller classes I round-robin students in the roles of actors and directors whereas with larger classes, or tighter time constraints, I allow some students to direct and others to act. Often the plays I select are short enough that one class period is sufficient for rehearsal time.

If I have the luxury to devote more than one class session to rehearsal, I invite small audiences that may consist of another class, the students' friends and family, or administrators. Creative writing students with no previous directorial or acting experiences will inevitably struggle but I emphasise that the point is not that plays have high production values, but rather that students gain new perspectives on stagecraft, which they can use to develop their own scripts.

One alternative to the traditional workshop format is allowing another student to direct a peer's play. Impromptu staged readings, in which different students each take parts, are helpful if time limitations do not permit more extensive productions. However, by allocating just one class for rehearsal time or assigning it as a group homework project, playwrights will get to see some possibilities and pitfalls of a production.

Sometimes only a few scripts can be selected so choosing plays that pose different staging requirements often benefits the rest of the class. After a performance, I encourage a 'talk-back' in which actors, directors, playwrights, and audience members engage in a question-and-answer session. It is important to discuss the production process to let the playwright understand the choices made in the development of the script.

The objective

Although directing is an interpretive activity, a brief experience directing a short, minimalist play can have a profound impact on students' ability to envision scripts as performances, and hence their competency as creative writers for the stage.

By beginning with materials and routines that emphasise the spectacle, students will become more sensitive to how scripts incorporate important theatrical elements such as action, ritual, song, space, lighting, costumes, and sound effects. Moreover, by familiarising students with older, foreign, avant-garde, or non-Western theatrical traditions, their scripts will not take certain modern dramaturgical, filmic, or televisual conventions for granted.

Producing student scripts in the classroom will also encourage them to think of their texts with the stage in mind and to literally see the results of their work. By using hands-on activities and staging unconventional plays, even those students who prefer to write more realistic drama will learn to write plays that are anything but conventional.

Contributor: Will Cordeiro

My name is Will Cordeiro. My name at birth was Billy Joe Bush, though this has been legally changed to William Joseph Cordeiro. I currently live in 'gorgeous' Ithaca, New York, among several waterfalls. I write poems, essays, and plays besides dabbling in other genres. I recommend that you read David Mamet's *Three uses of the knife*. Ask me if you need information on getting around Brooklyn. I can't help you with fixing (or even driving) a car. You'd never know I once grew a prize-winning pumpkin if I didn't tell you.

33

Exploring multiple viewpoints to create compelling narratives

Introduction
Exploring and developing a narrative from multiple viewpoints is an effective means of adding gravitas and fizz.

There are a number of ways to achieve this – for example, a single tale told by a range of sometimes conflicting first person voices, and with them perspectives, as in the case of Barbara Kingsolver's *The poisonwood bible* or Ali Smith's *The accidental*. However, a third person narrative, in which insight is given into the intimate sensibilities and personal motivations of various characters – including the least sympathetic – also makes for a provocative and intriguing read.

The following two short exercises are designed to help students in a creative writing class to begin to imagine and experiment with multiple viewpoints. Students may choose to include all of these viewpoints in their final story or they may choose to use the exercises simply to deepen their understanding of their characters, and help ensure a richer tale is told.

Exercise 1: one event, many tales
Students are told to imagine that two (or more) of their characters have experienced a single event. This could be something specific to each student's individual narrative in progress, or an event chosen for the class by the lecturer,

such as a wedding, a funeral, or a birth. Once the event and characters are decided upon, set the clock to four minutes. The aim is for students to do a freewrite in which they imagine that event through each of their chosen characters' eyes. Aim for four minutes per character, plus two minutes re-reading and 'resting' time between characters.

As a general rule I encourage students to do this exercise in the first person, as voice is arguably the most essential aspect of character. I have certainly found with my own teaching and writing that once one has discovered the voice of a character, one is well on the way to discovering everything else. However, if students prefer to write in the third person, that is fine too.

After the freewrite, students can be given another ten minutes to re-read and refine their work before moving on to Exercise 2.

THE OBJECTIVE
The aim of this exercise is to inspire students to consider the provocative, creative and moral possibilities of a narrative shaped by a range of perceptions and personalities.

Exercise 2: in conversation
This exercise can be adapted to a number of scenarios, such as a telephone conversation, an exchange of emails, letters, faxes or even texts. The conversation should revolve around the same event that was the spark for Exercise 1 and use the same characters, but this time the characters are interacting directly with others in a shared experience.

Once again I find that a freewrite works well to get the creative ball rolling. This should be about four minutes long, with students aiming to produce at least half a page of writing if it is a telephone conversation or collection of texts, or two sets of exchanges if emails or letters.

After the freewrite students should spend time refining and editing these exchanges, with reading them to the group being an optional extra to round off the exercise.

THE OBJECTIVE
From this exercise students will learn more about how their characters interact with one another, i.e., their relationships, possible undercurrents, silences and tensions. It also has the potential to act as a catalyst for narrative development as students apply their revelations about their characters' relationships to plot.

Contributor: Meg Vandermerwe
I was named after one of the sisters in Louisa May Alcott's *Little women*, although I'm not much like my namesake. I live in South Africa in the shadow of Table Mountain and write short stories and novels as well as journalism and academic non-fiction. I lecture at the University of the Western Cape. I recommend you read 'Responsibility' from Grace Paley's *Begin again: collected poems*. Ask me about making your own apple cider. I can't help with power tools. If I didn't tell you, you would never know that I am an animal whisperer.

34

Teaching the critical reflective essay

Introduction
The critical reflective essay (CRE) has become an increasingly popular tool in the creative writing assessment toolkit over the last decade. However, it is not always clear to students – or lecturers! – why it is set, or how to approach it.

One of the most challenging aspects of the CRE for students is its hybrid nature – an academic essay where they are allowed to use 'I', something students may well have been expressly taught not to do in their previous academic studies. As it can take time for students to assimilate the basic concepts of both critical reflection and critical reflective essays, it's probably best to teach the CRE over several classes, to allow students to develop and further build on their knowledge.

The exercise
This three-part exercise is taught in stages at the relevant points in the term.

STAGE 1 (WEEK 1 OR 2)
Ask the students to keep an informal journal of between 500–800 words per week in which to record how they go about building up their final writing portfolio for this course module. It's important to stress that you will not be looking at the journal, that it is purely for the students'

own reference. However, they will need to bring it to class later in the term.

STAGE 2 (WEEK 7 OF A 10-WEEK TERM)

Pre-teaching

At the end of the previous week, ask students to bring in an example of a 'standard' academic essay they have previously written, such as a school essay. If your students are not straight out of school you could supply them with a template essay. However, older students are more likely to be familiar with 'standard' academic essay format in any case.

In class

Show students an example of a good CRE in class. Allow them time to look over this. Then ask them to re-read the academic essay they have brought with them to class. Once they have done this, ask them to identify in pairs or small groups the similarities/differences between the two types of essays. Draw a vertical line down the middle of the board, head one section 'Same', the other 'Different', then ask the students to feed back their lists of similarities and differences and write these up on the board under the relevant heading.

Students will usually say things like 'the format' or 'beginning, middle and end', 'bibliography and footnotes' for similarities, and 'use of the first person', 'not given a proper title in a CRE' and 'you're allowed to focus on your own thoughts in a critical reflective essay' as differences.

However, do encourage them to think about the following:
- *stance* in each type of essay;
- *objectivity* and whether – and how – it is possible to

be critically detached when discussing your own work;
- the *purpose* of each essay;
- the essay *form* in each case;
- the type of *language* used in each essay.

At the end of this session, summarise the points covered then ask the students to take down the list of similarities and differences on the board, and bring it to class next week. Ask them also to bring in a piece of narrative written in the first person for the following week's class. It can be something from a magazine, such as a 'readers' true stories'-type article, a personal narrative, a section of an autobiography, a police witness statement – anything they like, so long as it is in the first person.

Finally, ask the students to bring in the journal they have been keeping since the beginning of term to use in next week's class.

STAGE 3 (WEEK 8)

Going round the class, ask students what kind of 'I' narrative they have brought in. Ask for volunteers to read theirs aloud. After each one, ask the rest of the group what they think the purpose of the narrative is. When all the volunteers have read, ask the students to work in pairs again and consider how the language of the narrative relates to the purpose the class identified. Then in the whole group, ask them to share their ideas and give specific examples. You can write some of these on the board.

Now ask the students to bring out i) the notes they made the previous week on the similarities/differences between the critical reflective essay and standard academic essays, ii) their journals. Ask them to discuss in small groups the

147

purpose of the CRE vis-à-vis the purpose of their journal. Encourage students to give examples from their own journals, of stance and how this relates to purpose, and to consider *objectivity* and *form*. Finally, ask them to think about *language* – specifically how, and why, the language in a journal is different from that of a critical reflective essay.

Finally, sum up the ideas covered in class, then ask students to refer back to the points covered in stages 2 and 3 and to attempt the first draft of a critical reflective essay for the following week, based on their experience of building up a writing portfolio for this module.

The objective
This three-part exercise aims to help students become more aware of what critical reflective essays are – and are not – by considering the differences and similarities between CREs and 'normal' academic essays. It also aims to teach students how to differentiate between self-reflection and self-absorption – often a challenge in the age of the celebrity 'confessional'.

Contributor: Sharon Norris
I was christened Sharon Rose, after my mum's dead sister's favourite hymn, but my dad, who has only one Christian name, decided I too should only have one, so I'm just known as 'Sharon'. I recommend *Inventing the truth: the art and craft of memoir* edited by William Zinsser. I write non-fiction. When I'm not writing, I like to sleep. Ask me if you need information on the Booker Prize, but not maths. If I didn't tell you, you'd never know I won first prize in a Gaelic music festival even though I don't speak Gaelic.

35

How to write a bad poem

Introduction

My goal in introducing a workshop on how to write bad poetry is two-fold: to help students new to the workshop setting to relax and enjoy the experience, and to give the class a common vocabulary in order to discuss each others' poems.

Obviously, I want my students to write good poems eventually. But in order to write well, it's necessary to first give themselves permission to make mistakes. Deliberately writing badly can take the pressure off and allow them to enjoy the process. Furthermore, in learning the elements that are found in bad poems, students gain the confidence to ensure that these elements won't appear in their good poems.

I teach this class early in the course, preferably so that it results in the first poem that my students write. I find it especially useful with students who haven't written or discussed poetry before or who have written poetry but have never attended a class or a workshop where their poetry is discussed.

The exercise

The students are provided with a list of bad poetry features. The following list can be adapted to suit the ability level of the students.

ELEMENTS OF BAD POEMS
Incorrect spelling
Bad grammar
Incorrect or confusing word usage
Inversion
Reversing words in a line for the sole reason of forcing a rhyme
Example: The feast ate they/at the break of day.
Poetic diction
Language that is only used for the sake of sounding poetic.
Example: Yon hill is a haven.
Archaic terms
Language that sounds as if it is from the middle ages.
Example: Thy head is thine/ but thy heart is mine.
Clichés
Phrases and words that have been overused.
Examples: 'you are in my heart' and 'love is blind'.
Informational language
Passive verbs
Verbs that require 'helping' words like 'has been' and 'was'.
Example: 'The fire was put out by the fireman' is passive.
'The fireman put out the fire' is active.
Overuse of adverbs and adjectives
a) The use of multiple adverbs or adjectives for a single noun or verb.
Example: The big, blond, ungainly boy
b) The use of an adverb or adjective to bolster a weak noun or verb.
Examples: 'ran fast' – a stronger verb, like 'dashed' or 'sped', would be better;
'male cat' – a stronger noun, like 'tom', would be better.
Abstract rather than concrete nouns
Examples: 'heaven', 'death', and 'freedom' are abstract; 'desk', 'man', and 'cow' are concrete.
Sentimentality

Starting the exercise

I tell the students that they are going to write incredibly bad poems, that the goal is to make them truly awful. Then I assure them that they won't have to share their poem with the class unless they want to.

As we discuss the list, I make it a point to tell the students that any of these elements, if used deliberately and consistently for a specific effect, can be part of a good poem. However, they're more often used carelessly or by accident and that's what makes for a bad poem. Depending on the time available and the needs of the students, I break up the discussion of specific bad elements with activities. For instance, when discussing abstract and concrete nouns, I write 'abstract' on one half of the board and 'concrete' on the other. I then invite students to come to the board a put a noun under one or both entries – if necessary, this can lead to a discussion on why abstract nouns in poetry are best avoided.

Once we've discussed the list of bad poem elements, I give the students ten minutes to write a poem using as many of the elements that we've discussed as possible. After they've written their poems, I offer to let them read the poems to the class and remind them that they can throw their poem in the trash immediately if they prefer. Most students choose to read, and even reluctant students will often retrieve their poem from the trash in order to amuse the class with how badly they've written. After everyone who wants to read has done so, we ceremonially crumple up the papers and toss them in the trash can.

The length of this exercise can be tailored to the age and ability level of the students. It also works well over two class periods.

The handout could be replaced with a list on the board. However, using the handout does save time students would spend noting the points down.

The objective

The exercise helps to promote a supportive atmosphere as students cheer on each other's efforts to write badly. As the poems are read amidst a great deal of laughter, students also tend to be more relaxed with each other. The supportive atmosphere carries over into later classes when students critique each other's work. The exercise also helps students find a place to start with critiques because they have a written list of the mechanical aspects of the poem to consider. They can compare their own poems against the list to minimise errors before reading. As students discover grammatical or poetic traps in their own writing, I encourage them to add to the list.

Students who are hesitant to read because of their own perfectionism or fear of classmates' responses will often volunteer to read their bad poems. This allows them to establish a greater comfort with reading and encourages them to read again in subsequent sessions. Having established a common language, less time in subsequent classes can be spent on mechanics and more time can be given to the expressive elements of the poem.

Contributor: Allene Nichols

My full name is Allene Rasmussen Nichols. 'Allene' is pronounced like 'Alan', but with a long 'e'. I live in Dallas Texas, where the only Cowboys there are wear American football uniforms. I write poetry and stage plays. I recommend *How to read a poem* by Burton Raffel. When

I'm not writing, I like photography and gardening. Ask me if you need information on teaching gifted or special needs students. I can't help you with fashion or shopping. If I didn't tell you, you'd never know that I used to work as a computer programmer.

36

Considering connotation: the impact and implications of language in poetry

Introduction

Although various aspects of poetry are considered in teaching creative writing, in my experience connotation receives attention mainly 'by-the-way' in discussion of rhyme, rhythm, form, etc. The particular meanings and associations attached to the language that poets use consist of what the poet her/himself brings from personal life experiences as well as those brought to the poems by every individual that reads them. Poets might not weigh all the possible connotations of each word as they write but, during the redrafting process, it is sometimes helpful to reconsider the implications of certain words. This can enhance the way that poems communicate on more than one level.

This exercise gives focus to underlying meanings of language and works well before other exercises that focus on poetic devices such as metaphor, alliteration and assonance, rhyme and rhythm, etc. It provides a practical way of introducing the importance of considering connotation because it demonstrates the impact and complexities of cultural and personal meanings and associations.

The exercise

STAGE 1: WHOLE GROUP

I introduce the exercise by explaining that even in casual communication, people sometimes understand something different from what the speaker or writer intended or, on the other hand, realise that their own words have been differently interpreted. I clarify that the purpose of the exercise is to help students to explore the implications of this, and to become more aware of how language works in poetry.

I ask them to consider a word that is not particularly emotive as an example, and find that 'bicycle' works well here; students think about bicycles in a general way first and make notes about appearance, different types, how they work, historical factors, and so on.

I then prompt them to think about their individual experiences of bicycles, for example, their first bike, when they learned to ride it or, if they did not have a bike, why that was, whether they like or dislike them, and to what degree. I also ask if they have any thoughts about using the full word or the shortened term.

This leads to discussion about particular people that bicycles remind the students of and, finally, any emotions that have arisen. I sometimes need to prompt them to be explicit about emotions they have mentioned implicitly; for example, excitement, freedom, fun, fear, etc.

I follow this pattern with another very different word, such as 'frog', starting with general points and moving on to individual experiences. This word is chosen to to generate a different discussion; for example, of nature in relation to collecting tadpoles, but also the dimension of fairytales can be introduced.

STAGE 2: INDIVIDUALLY
The students head two columns on a piece of paper: one heading is 'General' and the other 'Personal'. I explain

155

that the first refers to our wider society and culture, and the second to thoughts that are particular to individuals and their own experiences and personalities. I allow five minutes to consider each of seven words in turn and list, under each heading, all the connotations they can think of.

STAGE 3: WHOLE GROUP

Then students take each word in turn, sharing ideas around the group. I ask students to share any thoughts that arise about, for example, similarities and differences between individuals, cultural issues, variations in complexity between one word and another, meanings shared in one generation that are different in another, etc. It is not until this point that I reveal that the words are taken from a specific poem, and I read it to the group. I encourage discussion about whether individuals have heard or read the poem before and, importantly, what difference that makes when considering the connotations.

CHOOSING POEMS

While I explain that 'connotation' means the associations and ideas attached to a word or phrase, I make sure that students are not aware that words selected in stage 2 of the exercise are quoted from a poem because that will detract from their freedom to explore them as individual words.

However, it is important that the words are taken from a poem in order to illustrate the point that many associations are brought to the writing and reading of poetry. The poem must be one that students are likely to have read or heard, but not one that is immediately identifiable through its use of language, such as, 'tyger'/'burning'/'chain', etc.

Three poems that I find useful are:
'The lake isle of Innisfree', by W.B. Yeats
Suggested words: bee, cabin, glow, lake, pavement, veil, wings;
'Do not go gentle into that good night', by Dylan Thomas
Suggested words: age, frail, grave, height, meteor, sang, wave;
'Valentine', by Carol Ann Duffy
Suggested words: cute, cling, fierce, grief, moon, platinum, shrink.

FOLLOW-UP EXERCISE OR HOMEWORK
Students are asked to choose one word from the given list of seven as a title or theme and write a poem of twelve lines. Afterwards – and only once the poem is complete – they should consider what they bring to the language of their poem and what others might bring to reading it. They should come to the next meeting prepared to discuss this as a group.

The objective
To raise student writers' awareness of the impact of connotation through practical exercises, discussion and sharing experience with others for diversity and new ideas.

Contributor: Lesley Burt
My mother named me simply because she liked the name. Spelling mattered: the 'boys' version is Leslie, so I learned early to spell my name immediately after giving it, and still do. I write poetry, which has been published in magazines, online and in a book called *Framed and juxtaposed*. I recommend that you read *52 ways of looking at a poem*

by Ruth Padel. Ask me if you need information on social work with people who have learning disabilities. I can't help you with maths or sports. If I didn't tell you, you would never know that I do a lot of knitting.

37

Whatever!: exploring the 'authentic voice' in young-adult fiction

Introduction

One of the more challenging aspects of writing is finding an 'authentic voice', in particular when writing books for young adults. In terms of young adult fiction, I consider an authentic voice to be one that teenage readers can empathise with and that will engage them, rather than losing their interest. Research is one approach to achieving the authentic voice as it can assist the writer to get inside the head of a fifteen year old. The trick is to ensure that this research isn't too obvious but is subsumed into the text so that the reader merely perceives a depth of narrative and that there are no screaming howlers that make them put the book down or misinform them. This research can take many forms, including 'people watching' and using the Internet. Internet research can explore all sorts of sites from blogs to government sponsored ones and, therefore, offer both casual and more formal voices.

For the lecturer working with a large number of students who are still young adults themselves, approaching this narrative voice provides additional challenges. The young adult culture shifts rapidly so though some of your students may still be young adults they may have lost touch with what it is like to be a younger teenager. This exercise is one I have used successfully to get the students to consider what makes the 'authentic voice' and how to write a story that a teenager can empathise with whilst considering what sort of message they are going to give their reader.

Teaching creative writing

Lecturer preparation

1. Collect a selection of teenage magazines. Most will be aimed at girls so it's important to include some aimed at boys, though finding them can be difficult. Go through these and cut out anything interesting or challenging. These can be from problem pages, articles, pictures, quizzes or even adverts. Place all the cuttings into a large envelope.

2. Photocopy a couple of pages from several examples of fiction aimed at young adults focusing on the issues they deal with or that you wish to discuss. You don't need many as the students will have limited time to read them so make sure they are relevant and short. Consider including material for discussion on whether or not there are subjects that shouldn't be written about, and why.

Student preparation

The session beforehand, ask your students to 'teenager watch' when they are out and in particular suggest they pay attention to mannerisms, the language used and interactions between people. Ideally this should not just be among their friends. It's important to draw attention to personal safety when doing this preparation. Encourage them to watch TV programmes aimed at teenagers too. This is particularly useful if you have older students who would feel uncomfortable hanging around teenage haunts.

Reading and discussion exercise

Give the fiction handouts to all the students and allow enough time for them to read them all. Having done that, discuss how young adult fiction deals with issues and

160

whether the examples read had this perceived 'authentic voice'. Ask the students if they would they do it differently. Follow straight on to the writing exercise as this allows them an opportunity to show how they would do it and also to find out through practice if their way would work.

Writing exercise
This can be done in class as a short piece and/or it can be set as further homework. A short piece started in class could be a stand-alone exercise or developed and researched ready for workshopping the following week and that could also form the basis of an assignment.

Spread the magazine cuttings out in front of the students. Give them a few minutes to look at them. Then ask them to select one they can use as either a starting point where the story may go in any direction or as an inspiration where the whole story is based around the cutting. If you want them to have a more random and limited choice ask them to take one unseen from the envelope. By using the magazine cuttings, there is an opportunity for them to write about teenage issues and you may want them to consider how they are going to do this and what message they want to give to the reader.

Give them fifteen minutes to write their initial thoughts and develop them into a coherent narrative. Ask all or some of the students to read out their work to the class. Each piece can be followed by feedback from both the lecturer and students focusing, at this stage, on how well they have dealt with the narrative. Discuss how the stories could be developed and the potential pitfalls.

For homework, ask them to develop the piece further by undertaking research – you may want to discuss the sort of research they could do. They should be aiming to achieve an authentic voice by using their research to create a voice that teenagers can empathise with and is not overly didactic.

The objective

The objective of the exercise is to raise awareness and understanding of the issues involved in writing realist young adult fiction. It gives the student an opportunity to create their own authentic voice as a writer. The exercise also encourages the student to understand the importance of research and getting the details right, particularly when dealing with teenage issues.

Contributor: Vanessa Harbour

My name is Vanessa, which was invented by Jonathan Swift and used by James Joyce in *Finnegans wake*. I write fiction for children aimed at 7+ and YAF. I edit an ejournal which can be found at www.write4children.org. I recommend Andrew Melrose's *Write for children*. When I am not writing, I concentrate on living life to the full. Ask me if you need information on sex, drugs and alcohol in teenage fiction. I can't help you with physics or French. If I didn't tell you, you'd never know that I don't eat.

38

'Give and take': getting a stage play on its feet

Introduction

Audiences rarely read plays; they go to see them. A play text is thus a blueprint for a production. One of the first things a director is likely to do during the rehearsal process is to 'get the play up on its feet' in order to see how well it works on the stage once the characters are physically interacting with one another. The movements the actors make on the stage will be carefully choreographed, or 'blocked', in order to maximise the dramatic potential of the script. This process can be illuminating for the playwright, as she suddenly realises that certain scenes don't work in quite the way she had imagined, or she starts to see new dramatic potential that she has failed to exploit.

Creative writing courses often neglect this important aspect of writing for the stage. The following exercise aims to give the creative writing student a new insight into how their play might work more effectively on the stage, as opposed to on the page.

The exercise

Ideally the students will take turns playing the characters in one another's scripts, though it is technically possible for a single playwright to take each role in turn and still gain some new perspective on the play.

Mark out a space that can be used to represent the stage, and assign to each student the role of one of the characters in the play. Begin the exercise by giving one of the participants an object of some sort – a tennis ball, a pen, a book, whatever you happen to have at hand. Ask the participants to adopt a starting position anywhere in the space you have marked as 'the stage'. It may prove helpful to position chairs within the space, so that the characters can place their objects upon them.

The character with the first line of dialogue should take the object from whichever character is holding it, and place it at a random spot upon the stage, or give it to another character, delivering their lines as they do so.

The next character should then deliver their lines and simultaneously retrieve the object from its current position, or take the object from another character, and again place the object in a new position on the stage, or give it to another character.

Students should be instructed to ignore any stage direction in the script for the duration of the exercise. Each character should be free to move to whichever area of the stage feels most natural for them in order to acquire or dispose of the object.

By improvising movements without regard to the words the characters are speaking, students can begin to think about the script in a new way. The focus shifts to the physicality of the scenes, and to how the physical movements of the characters might best facilitate the playwright's aims in the scene. Once a particular movement, or set of movements, is found to be effective, the writer can look at the motivations of the characters in the scene, and at what the impetus might be for them to move to a particular place at a particular time.

EXPLORING DIFFERENT STAGE CONFIGURATIONS

The stage space can be envisioned – by both those participating and observing – as a proscenium arch, a thrust stage or a theatre-in-the-round. You might discuss how the different stage configurations affect the perception of the events on the stage, depending upon where the characters move. On a standard proscenium arch stage, for example, the downstage centre of the space will generally be perceived as the area where characters have the most immediate connection with the audience. Key dramatic moments will usually be most effective when played out here, and thus the challenge for the playwright is to ensure that the characters can move easily to this area of the stage for these moments. The dynamic between the audience and the actor(s) changes when the stage is configured as a theatre-in-the-round, and ideally a play script should be flexible enough to work effectively regardless of the stage configuration.

You can also help students assess the practicality and effectiveness of characters' exits and entrances with this exercise. The emphasis throughout should be on experimentation and discussion, getting the students to try out different character movements to see what appears to work, and what, if anything, needs to be improved upon.

The objective

The exercise should get students thinking about the broader subject of how the stage space works in terms of connecting the audience with the actors. The students can see and hear for themselves the difference between a speech delivered from the back left corner of the stage and one delivered front centre.

The object of the exercise is not to fix movements ahead of any production of the script, but to allow the playwright to think of how their script might work for actors, a production crew and an audience, rather than how it might work for a reader. This key shift in thinking can often be helpful for students, particularly if they come to stage writing from a prose background.

Contributor: Paul Lucas

My full name is Paul Gerard. I was named after the saint, and an uncle who fits carpets in Dublin, both of whom experienced 'road to Damascus' conversions. I write stage plays – comedies, ostensibly, which have been performed in Edinburgh, Birmingham, Coventry, Scarborough and the West End. I recommend *Playwrights at work (The Paris Review interviews)* edited by George Plimpton. I can't help you with free form jazz or Angry Birds. If I didn't tell you, you would never know that I'm a trained pyrotechnician.

39

Start where you are: read what you know

Introduction
Not all students come to a writing class equipped with the critical skills required to give or receive feedback on writing. Face to face these skills can be taught relatively simply. But not all writing students are in a position to attend a face-to-face writing class. In the following exercises, I focus on instilling the value of reading as a writer to beginning writing students. The aim is to assist those students studying remotely, whether on a one-to-one basis, or with access to an online forum, to develop those critical skills starting with texts they are already familiar with.

When I was a remote student studying alone at home with nobody over the age of five years available to critique my writing, I began to develop exercises similar to those outlined. Working it out as I went along, I read widely and examined texts for specific purposes, modelled my first drafts around those purposes, and wrote short analyses of the techniques used by both the published writer and me, the student. I became more objective and moved beyond the 'like/didn't like' response common to early writing students.

In the early stages of a course, I now adopt similar strategies linked to reading, engaging critically, and examining the works of the students' own choosing. We then collaborate to devise short 'modelling exercises' based on student responses to specific questions about aspects of the writer's craft. These exercises serve as a blueprint rather than specific formulaic exercises and flexibility is necessary to this approach.

The exercises
Class 1

In early communications (generally via email, though sometimes by online chat or Skype), we establish what each student reads, how often, and why they choose to read the books and authors they do. We address too, the differences between reading as a reader and reading as a writer. I ask the students to select a short story or sample chapter of writing, ideally one discussed in communications.

I then ask each student to think in general terms about their selection and make some notes. What specifically interests them? Is it the language, the pace, the suspense, the description, imagery, etc.? Depending on the focus of the next class, I request some specific written responses. For example, if looking at structure I might ask them to consider methods of narrative construction in their selected piece. If looking at memory or flashback, similarly, I'd ask them to examine the ways in which these are used.

In an online group class, this can be done via message boards or group emails. By establishing a sense of who classmates are and where their reading interests lie, it also serves as an ice-breaker. However, it works well in a one-to-one situation too, helping the student gain confidence in sharing ideas and valuing their own opinions when working alone with a lecturer.

CLASS 2

Each student sends me his or her responses to questions posed in our previous session by email. We then discuss the readings, via whichever means we've chosen, with emphasis on those responses. I find in the early stages that discussing a reading of their own choice establishes ownership of their programme of study. It also assists less confident students to respond to works of their own choosing before addressing those I later encourage them to consider in terms of literary taste and style. Together, we devise individualised writing exercises based on their responses. For example, if one student was particularly taken with the way his writer used first person and a memory of a particular childhood experience to lead the character into a harrowing flashback scene, he might elect to attempt one of his own, adapting those techniques he admired.

I ask each student to work on the exercise and to then write a brief analysis of their writing before the next session. Both of these are emailed to me. I provide feedback on each part of the exercise, focusing at this early stage on the analysis rather than the creative writing exercise itself. We then establish the focus of the next class – for example, the relationship between action and description – and I ask the students to select a piece of writing, examine the text, write a short response to the focus questions and send it to me.

In the next session, we discuss that response, devise a creative writing exercise based on the established focus, and so it continues. Within a few sessions, students are generally able to examine their own written work more rigorously.

The objective

Engaging students and encouraging them to read, reflect and engage critically with the writings they enjoy, brings them to the learning process with a sense of empowerment. While they may start by analysing the latest popular fiction or 'lowbrow' creative material, they generally quickly develop the confidence in applying those strategies they identify to more literary texts and to their own writing.

The approach further adds value in helping instill a strong work ethic for writers. Responsibility for regular reading and writing is placed on the individual and reflective analysis of their own and others' works, whether of their own choosing or 'set' reading, becomes an ongoing part of their writerly development.

Contributor: Michelle M. Crawford

I always thought that I was named after that famous Beatles song, but I discovered when I was a teenager that I was here first. I currently live in Perth, Western Australia and spent much of my adult years living in a desert town in the remote north of the state. I mainly write fiction, poetry and non-fiction. I recommend *The writing book* by Kate Grenville. When not writing, I attempt to learn to read and speak French. If I didn't tell you, you'd never know that I helped deliver my daughter's first baby last year.

40

Writing suspense(fully)

Introduction
Alfred Hitchcock, no mere amateur in creating suspense, was fond of pointing out that if an audience is aware that a time bomb has been hidden under the dinner table, and the characters are not, then every moment of what could be viewed as a fairly typical, even monotonous scene – a simple dinner party – becomes riveting. In this case, suspense is predicated on a sense of *knowing* – what an audience can see versus what the character can – and, as passive voyeurs of a film, this knowledge can create tension as we watch the scene unfold.

Writing, however, requires a more active participant. Readers are not passive like viewers; the act of reading itself is often propelled by the discovery of information, almost always at the same time as the protagonist/ narrator. Thus it is important for a writer to understand the difference between creating *passive suspense* (as on film or in a drama) and *active suspense* (in a narrative) and the need to achieve tension in the reader to keep them turning the pages.

Many of my students enjoy writing genre fiction, and in many genres – mystery, horror, thriller, fantasy, science fiction – suspense can play a key role in developing the story. However, scenes of suspenseful writing can heighten tension and drama in any genre, whether attached to moments of fear, stress, or discovery. This exercise, then, is designed not only to furnish students with an understanding of how tension can be created in a text, but also to provide creative tools that could be used in any context.

The exercise

First, have your students select passages of suspenseful writing that they feel are successful to share with the class. Conversely, you may wish to bring these passages to class yourself from set reading materials for the course. Have your students examine these passages in small groups and ask them to specifically identify what writing techniques they spot that add to the piece's tension. Then discuss what they believe makes the passages particularly suspenseful.

Next, giving the handout below as a checklist, go over these six keys to writing a suspenseful passage in a story. Have your students identify those techniques they spot in the passages they brought to class. Remind them that a key to creating suspense is to balance these techniques with strong, descriptive writing, as too much of any technique can turn writing into parody.

SIX KEYS TO WRITING SUSPENSE(FULLY)

1. Keep extraneous words to a minimum. Focus on good, strong verbs.
2. Use common vocabulary (now is not the time to show off your perspicacity!)
3. The language should reflect the action of the piece. It should be purposeful and to the point. Don't delay action – action is the engine that drives the narrative forward. Do delay endings – making the reader wait for the climax of the scene is always impactful.

---

4. Short sentences increase the rhythm of the piece, while long sentences slow it down. Moving the rhythm from fast to slow can intensify tension in a passage; disrupting the rhythm of a piece can add suspense.
5. The repetition of key words or phrases can also increase the pace for the reader.
6. For longer passages, moving back and forth between two vantage points can be effective. Writers can shift from one perspective to another. This is a technique borrowed from cinema. A famous silent film, *The perils of Pauline* (1914) includes a classic example of this. In the film, the heroine is tied to a set of train tracks. The hero tries desperately to save her while the train comes speeding down the tracks. You need not see the film to imagine the tension being created as the movie cuts swiftly between the heroine's screaming face, the hero speeding in, and the train charging ever closer, all creating suspense. Of course, shifts in point of view can be tricky for new writers – so it is important to make sure that this technique fits within the existing structure of your story.

Now ask your students to write their own suspense passage from the prompts below. While none of the prompts are inherently suspenseful, have them use the writing techniques outlined above to make them so:

- Mother bakes some chocolate-chip cookies;
- purchasing a goldfish at the pet store;
- making a dinner decision at a fast-food restaurant.

Complete the exercise with a read-round from volunteers and discussion of the techniques.

The objective

From this exercise students will be able to learn that *how* they write can be as important as *what* they write. They will practise specific techniques that will enable them to add suspense into anything they write, regardless of genre or even form (these techniques work for poetry as well as prose). They will also learn that part of writing is learning specific skills that all good writers should be able to call upon, if needed. Being able to write suspensefully will provide students with not only with a technique useful to all writers but also help them to recognise that the act of reading itself, with its active participant, differs from the passive act of viewing. This will, in turn, allow your students to gain a greater understanding of the subject matter they are studying.

Contributor: Michael G. Cornelius

My name is Michael Cornelius. I live in Pennsylvania, USA. I write speculative fiction, usually. I recommend David Starkey's *Creative writing: four genres in brief.* When I'm not writing, I like to lavish attention on a black pug named after church reformer John Knox – or on my spouse, whichever is handy. Ask me if you need information on girl detective books. But I'm no good with technology – I still can't get my iPod working. If I didn't tell you, you'd never know that my winning smile conceals an antisocial misanthrope – but now that I have, leave me alone.

41

Other talents: 'doing creative (writing)'

Introduction

Creative writing classes can easily spin by without the subject of creativity itself ever coming up. I think this is because we lecturers tend to be very creative people, and asking creative people about creativity is like asking a fish about water: it's hard to have any perspective on the stuff you're immersed in all the time.

Experienced creative people tend to think in terms of process: we know it helps to be in a certain room, or to write at a certain time of day. We know to avoid reading the news or thinking about our bank accounts.

But many students are still carving out an identity as a creative person. They aren't ready for process: they're still learning what it means to invent with language and create something others can enjoy. They are still learning what unique thing they have to offer that others might be interested in.

This is why I always devote a portion of class time to an open conversation about the many ways my students have been creative throughout their lives. The boundaries of art are surely debatable, but for the students' sake, I let the list be inclusive: if their activities have been even mildly creative, I call it so.

Try this in your own classes, and I bet you will discover, as I have, that your students have done all sorts of things, things you've never dreamed of doing, things they can tap into to write more interestingly for you and for each other.

The exercise

Set aside thirty to sixty minutes and ask them: who has made their own clothes? Who has played an instrument or sung in a choir? Who writes fan fiction? Who draws, or even just doodles cartoons? Who knits? Who folds origami? Who spent their childhood making monuments out of block sets? Sandcastles on the beach? Faces out of their plated food? Who makes videos for the internet? Music mixes for friends? Who takes photos of odd things they spot along the sidewalk or while shopping? Who has made a fake online profile? Who has made a website? Who likes to make posters for clubs? Who has come up with an idea for a whole new video game?

Let them brag, and laugh, and ask each other questions. The value of this conversation is intrinsic: when students start thinking of themselves as creative people, start counting all the creative things they've done throughout their lives, they gain confidence and are stronger inventors and creators.

But you can take it beyond the intrinsic: ask them how they can incorporate their other talents into their writing. Can they build an online profile for a character they've invented, or some grand historical figure? Use photos or drawings to accompany a story? Can they build a synaesthetic bridge between one art form and another? What would a story written in musical notation look like? What would a story inspired by knitting or origami-folding look like? Can your students get into the psychology of their computer game characters? They can make them leap and shoot fireballs, sure, but can they imagine the crushing ennui of a being who is a puppet, who relives the same sequences of events over and over, who dies time and again, only to wake and start all over again?

My favourite assignment, one that lets students bring their creativity from all realms of life, is to ask them to write a story that will fit on one side of one page – something that could be conceivably hung on a wall – in a way that will strike the reader visually and then tell a story upon closer inspection. Students can 'sketch' a picture/word story in charcoal or use their computer to generate images made of words (there are several free programs online to help them do this). Students with a background in crafts can make 3D sculptures covered in words or abstract art books.

The lecturer's willingness to say 'yes' to these experiments encourages the experimentation itself. Let ambitious ideas that seem difficult, maybe even bound for failure, go forward: sometimes they fail, yes, but they might fail beautifully or transform into something else entirely, and sometimes they succeed beyond the imagination. As the lecturer, it's important to never punish failure, only reward risk-taking.

Beginning creative writers need to discover that they have something unique to bring to writing, and that it is connected to their history of creativity, not just to their experiences putting words on a page. They need to feel free to try the scary or dangerous thing.

They must be free to risk disaster to tempt art.

The objective

The objectives of this assignment are three-fold:

Confidence building: by tapping into experiences and abilities particular to them, the students gain confidence, and can begin to see how they have something unique to offer in their creative work.

Group bonding: by letting the students share parts of their creative pasts with the group, this conversation and assignment helps them not just get to know one another, but get to know one another as creative people.

Creativity enhancing: the junctions between different forms of creativity can be particularly rich and energetic sources of material; students who might have believed that creative writing takes a particular, conventional form can be inspired to discover new forms.

Contributor: Amy Letter

My name is Amy Letter. Most Letters went into postal-delivery, but I decided to become a writer. I live in Fort Lauderdale, Florida, a subtropical swamp with a beach – here everything is dangerous: plants, animals, weather. Ask me if you need information on the physics of science fiction universes. I can't help you with fantasy universes. You'd never know if I didn't tell you that I love to play my baritone ukulele.

42

Fascinating rhythm: teaching songwriting – a multi-modal experience

Introduction

It is a measure of creative writing's development as an academic discipline that it has been able to embrace a range of sub-disciplines, including song/lyric writing. While the number of creative writing programmes offering courses in lyric writing is still relatively small, it is growing, reflecting the popularity of the subject with students and the fact that many students come to creative writing through songwriting.

Is a creative writing programme an appropriate context for learning song/lyric writing? My own answer to this is, 'Of course'. Like all genres of writing, it is concerned with a given form and specific writing context, and with the particular use of language required by the genre. The key difference between this and other types of creative writing, however, is that songs are 'multi-modal', that is, they use two channels – words and music – to convey meaning.

This exercise is all about a) increasing students' awareness of rhythm and stress patterns in both music and the spoken word, b) impressing on students that the successful lyricist needs to be aware of how each channel works and the relationship of the one to the other in song.

The exercise
STAGE 1
This exercise can either be used where students have already studied stress patterns in poetry, e.g. iambs, trochees, etc., or it may be used as an initial 'awareness-raising' activity.

Pre-teaching
You will need to prepare by a) recording a selection of musical 'snippets' and b) compiling a list of phrases for students to use. As far as the music's concerned, there is much to commend the use of well-known or traditional tunes, as part of what this exercise aims to do is to get students to listen in a different way, i.e. for patterns, rhythm, etc. The dafter the phrases the better, as you're looking at this point to break the associations between words and 'sense'.

In class
First of all, write a selection of phrases on the board that you already know match up with the musical examples you've selected and go over these with the students. Now play the musical 'snippets' several times. Next, divide students into pairs and ask them to match the music to the phrases. Make the point that they should be looking for stress patterns, no more. Musical examples could include:

a) The first line of 'The lass of Richmond Hill', (i.e. 'On Richmond Hill there lives a lass ...');

b) The first line of 'Ae fond kiss', (i.e. 'Ae fond kiss, and then we sever');

c) Any other well-known song the whole class is likely to be familiar with (e.g. 'Happy birthday').

Sample phrases for the above include: 'I've got nits but you've got dandruff ' – matches b); 'You've got to go to work today' – matches a).

FEEDBACK

Feed back and check they've got the right answer.

Did they manage to work it out? How? What you're looking for here is for students to recognise similarities in the stress patterns of the music and those of the words.

Suggest that if they're unsure in future, they might want to tap out the rhythm of the music or the words as this will help them to work out where the stresses come and how many there are. This is a good point at which to draw parallels with poetry if you want to.

STAGE 2

Drawing on the knowledge they have gained from stage 1, of how to identify where words and music do/don't match, now ask the students to suggest a section of music the whole class will know to match the following phrases:

a) 'I hate washing dishes

   I hate making wishes'

(Lots of potentials here, including Lady Gaga's 'Bad romance');

b) 'Just you wait till I tell everyone'

(Again, lots of potentials, e.g. Kylie Minogue's 'Can't get you out of my head').

FEEDBACK

List *all* the suggested matching tunes on the board and ask the rest of the class if they agree that these match the words.

Ask what elements of the words influenced students' choice of music. Here they may mention, in addition to rhythm, the stress on individual sounds – at this stage you can focus simply on whether these are 'consonants' or 'vowels'; but try to tease this out a little and encourage students to think about the nature of the consonants. Are they 'crisp' or 'heavy' sounds, etc., and the same for vowels; are they long, short, soft, etc.? Next, get students to focus on the rhythm.

STAGE 3

Now ask the class to make up their own music to fit the following phrases:

a) 'Couldn't you, please, just leave me alone?';

b) 'Transcendental meditation'.

FEEDBACK

Again, ask what elements of the words influenced students' choice of music.

If you know any phonetics, you could introduce the terms fricatives, liquids, dentals, etc., to enable students to further break down their analysis of word sounds.

Ask them to represent the rhythm of these two phrases, using — to represent a stress and ˘ to represent unstressed syllables.

STAGE 4

Listen to 'The black bear salute', track 4 on the album *Purely pipers* (students can find this album on Spotify).

Ask them to write lyrics to the section from 0:02 to 0:12.

Traditional Scottish music is useful for these sorts of exercises as it is particularly rhythmic. This could be done as a homework exercise for feedback and discussion at the next meeting.

FEEDBACK

Ask them to read out/sing their lyrics.

Ask the other students whether they fit. If not, why not?

Ask each student what influenced their choice of words.

The objective

The aim here is to develop students' awareness of:

- rhythm and stress in music and in normal speech patterns and in individual words;
- how intonational patterns, for example in the way we ask questions, may be replicated in music;
- the relationship of words to music, at the level of rhythm, tempo and the unique sounds of individual speech elements.

From the experience of analysing shorter sections and phrases, students should then be able to move on to writing lyrics for longer pieces of music, starting with whole verses, then eventually entire songs.

Having been given the chance to practise their skills in the above areas, students should be able both to analyse and to address particular problems presented by certain types of music.

Contributor: Sharon Norris

At primary school, a student teacher taught us about the Israelites. She told us to write our names backwards on rolled-up paper, like Hebrew scrolls. The student kept telling me mine was wrong. Eventually she shouted: 'No, Sirron – you're *still* not getting it right!' I recommend *Writing: self and reflexivity*, by Celia Hunt and Fiona Sampson. I write non-fiction. When I'm not writing, I like to travel. Ask me if you need information on Norway, but not Finland. I've never been there. If I didn't tell you, you'd never know I get pizza on prescription.

43

Leaving the comfort zone: against practicality and rationality

Introduction
The pleasure and enjoyment that can be attained when imagination is freely exercised is often neglected by beginner writers in their concerns over technique. One of the pleasures of writing poetry I try to share with my students is the opportunity to explore language that departs from practicality and rationality.

Leaving the linguistic comfort zone is particularly an issue for speakers or writers using English as a second language because their focus on grammatical accuracy is always prioritised. I have tried the following two exercises with my undergraduate students who are mainly from Hong Kong and China. As they are learning to be English teachers, I find them over-reliant on education theories and second language learning pedagogies. They are very often concerned with the practical and rational side of language and ignore their creative potential.

My aim is to use poetry as a prompt to encourage writers to discover what language can do otherwise.

Exercise 1
I ask each student in class to write down a noun of their choice on a small piece of paper and put it into a box or plastic bag. It can be a concrete or abstract noun, but words about seasons, emotions, or that can allow spontaneous imagination are preferred.

I use Bei Dao's 'Notes from the city of the sun' as a model, which consists of fourteen short segments, each titled with a common noun. I find Bei Dao's poetry is particularly useful with my students since it is widely read and discussed in Hong Kong. However, it has potential for use with students anywhere, not only because it deals with East–West identity/ cultural politics, but also because of its surrealistic edge. The verses tend to be metaphorical definitions of the noun given and can trigger different interpretations among readers.

The following examples are my own imitations of his style:

Youth
An enlarged ego
ditched into the trench
of ageing

Poverty
What you cannot hide
besides coughing
and love

Beauty
Universally accepted
currency

After a close reading of Bei Dao's verse, I invite each student to draw a noun from the bag and write a metaphorical definition of what the noun means to him/ her. Students need to be reminded not to be too logical in this exercise, or else their poems will read more like a dictionary entry. On the contrary, I encourage them to imitate the surrealistic touch in Dao's poems when they create a tiny narrative for a specific noun.

I often go on to compile a longer poem by collecting everyone's piece and, in order to enhance a collective sense of involvement, I might also participate in the writing process, depending on the time available and number in the group.

Exercise 2
Homolinguistic translation is fun because it allows the writer to re-create the content in a different discourse. I use this process by introducing my students to the Howard Moss version of Shakespeare's 'Shall I compare thee to a summer's day?', which 'translates' the romantic images into contemporary English. Moss maintains the rhyme scheme but has only thirteen lines, breaking with the convention of the 14-line sonnet. His treatment of this very familiar poem provides an opportunity to discuss language and form, which adds another element to the exercise.

After reading the two versions of the sonnet, both of which are easily found online, I follow the analysis of the poem with a brief discussion of the technical aspects of a sonnet and the ways Moss either breaks with or works within the tradition.

Once they start the rewriting process, students are free to regenerate the images in their own metaphors. I also encourage them to make use of rhyming dictionaries, in hard copy or online, to facilitate their writing process. I remind them that end-rhymes, like any other forms, do not necessarily impose restrictions on the author. On the contrary, they may be ways to uncover surprises.

The objective
The first exercise helps students to create their own short 'definition poem', which rejects the understanding of

nouns in the practical and rational sense. It also offers students a chance to use their imagination and express what the subject matter means to them. The second exercise allows students to understand the features of a sonnet and to work within the convention and break it at the same time.

Contributor: Nicholas Y.B. Wong
My name is Nicholas Y.B. Wong. I live in Hong Kong, but mostly in my own thoughts. I write poetry and like to experiment with different forms and contents – see http://nicholasybwong.weebly.com. I recommend *Ordinary genius: a guide for the poet within* by Kim Addonizio. Ask me if you need information on where to submit poems and get yourself known in the cyberspace. I can't help you with quitting smoking and coffee. If I didn't tell you, you'd never know that I love dogs more than humans. At home, I speak in Cantonese, my first language. Mostly, I don't speak at all.

44

Flights of fancy: writing from myth

Introduction

Classical myth makes good raw material for the creative writer and, reflectively treated, can inspire resonant fresh material that speaks to our own times. A common trap is simply to 'update' the story, with new names and setting but the same plot. A story drawing on Icarus and Daedalus, for example, need not include a father and son named Ian and Derek, or be about flying or a literal fall into the sea. Instead the challenge is to analyse the tale, extract the essence, and write something recognisably triggered by the original but saying something new – and not necessarily with a contemporary setting. The following exercise specifically addresses writing, but also foregrounds processes of interpretation and critical thinking.

The exercise

PREPARATORY STAGE

Start the exercise with the whole class for stage 1, and then subdivide it into small groups for the next two stages. I find a prose translation of Ovid such as Mary M. Innes's edition of *Metamorphoses* is best, as the narrative is immediately accessible.

Begin with a simple question, such as 'What is this story about?' Expect summaries, for example, 'Daedalus is an experimenter who makes wings out of feathers and wax for himself and his son; they both fly up but Icarus goes too close to the sun so his wings melt and he falls into the

sea.' Then ask what the story makes them think or feel.
This encourages a movement beyond the narrative. You
might get responses like, 'He should have listened to his
dad!', 'He got carried away, enjoying the experience', or,
'Daedalus probably blames himself', or 'Did he follow a
proper health and safety procedure?' or, 'It's a dream, isn't
it, to be able to fly?'

Then ask them how they would update it. You may
well get the Derek and Ian scenario, depending on the
cultural default; someone might think of Yves Rossy, the
pilot who has flown with real working wings; or pick up on
the health and safety comment, and suggest a factory that
makes flying kits for sport and leisure. This is somewhat too
literal and narrow, so ask them to ditch all the discussion
so far – it was just a preliminary exercise. Of course, they
won't really just forget like this: the desired effect is that
this stage is discarded on a conscious level, while it is in
fact kept in mind, to feed into the ensuing development
of ideas.

EXPLORATORY STAGE

This works particularly well if you split the class into small
groups of between three and six. Still working on Icarus,
give each group three pieces of card. Ask them to write
responses to the following three questions, one on each
card: What is the fear in this story? What is the hope? What
is the most significant detail? This formula works for most
stories.

You're aiming for more symbolic, less literal readings,
such as fears of dying, or of going too far, of your child
taking risks, of exploration, of divine wrath, of technology
or science, of recklessness, of being trapped by fate.

And hopes, for example, might be of escaping from confinement, returning home, problem-solving, thrill-seeking, going further than Dad, passing on something to your son, using technology to improve life and transcend human limitation.

Finally, significant details might be wax and feathers, wings, the old man's tears, the dark blue sea, the ploughman. Allow a time-limit for this exercise, then ask the students to share their answers with the class. It is important to have this stage of interaction, because it should illustrate the many different ways in which the story can be interpreted; the many dimensions of meaning; and the ways in which the story connects with our own preoccupations and dreams.

WRITING STAGE

After this, mix up the pieces of card, and redistribute them, so each group ends up with a fresh three, each with a fear, a hope or a detail on it. Ask them once more to forget about all the previous discussion – again a disingenuous instruction, since of course they can't forget about it but are nevertheless encouraged to move on from it. Then ask each student to use the three items on their group's list to write a fresh story or poem, including the three elements, but not consciously based on the Icarus story. At the end of the class, ask for volunteers to read out what they have written, and invite discussion on ways in which the new stories/poems dialogue with the Icarus story.

The objective

The point of this class is twofold: to engage students in the process of writing from sources, and to serve as a study of hermeneutics. By engaging in writing students will have produced original creative work, and gained a greater understanding of how such writing – and perhaps all writing – works. Myth is a particularly resonant example, but the students should potentially have learnt something about the processes of interpretation in general in literary studies, and the ways in which our own concerns direct our location of meanings in texts.

Contributor: Amina Alyal

I was named after the heroine of a Bellini opera. I write both scholarly texts and poetry, which you can read about at http://www.leedstrinity.ac.uk/departments/english/staff/Pages/Alyal.aspx. I recommend that you read *Myth and creative writing* by Adrian May. When I'm not writing, I like to cook. Ask me if you need information on Persian art or obscure Elizabethan poets. I can't help you with football or TV reality shows. You'd never have known if I hadn't told you, that I'm always listening to the Dubliners.

45

Found poetry workshop

Introduction
This hands-on found poetry exercise has its roots in the Dadaist movement and Tristan Tzara's cut up technique. Using the Dada technique, a cut up poem is constructed by cutting up a piece of writing and drawing words out of a box or bag to create the poem. History has Tzara using a hat.

While my students always enjoyed the classroom discussion of the cut up's background, and learning about writers such as William Burroughs who had employed the technique, the exercise really didn't resonate with them. After changing the procedure a bit, I found that the students appreciated having more control over the narrative, and that the act of actually writing, choosing and placing the words, also made them more engaged and creative.

This exercise is especially good for students who are visually oriented. I have found that they are more likely to experiment with shapes and unusual line lengths and breaks than they would if writing a poem on a computer or by hand.

The exercise
I use a whole class period to hold the workshop. I have found that it works best when I have a large block of time, such as an evening class. For shorter class periods, it is best to prep the group during the class prior so they don't waste time settling in to the exercise.

For this exercise, I encourage the students to find a magazine article, news story, or advertisement that they would like to transform. In addition, I ask them to bring a glue stick and scissors. I also bring additional magazines, newspapers, glue sticks and scissors so there are enough to go around. Occasionally even those who show up prepared will be inspired by something they see in class and use one of the magazines I provided.

Then I have them start cutting. I never set any limits on the size and kind of poem they can create. I've found they often think of things I've never seen before. I also let them decide how much they want to challenge themselves, such as trying to write a love poem from a news story about war or crafting a simple haiku.

The only rule I have regarding this exercise is that they stick with the one article, ad, or essay. I have found it is important for them to limit their lexicon to the language in the written piece. If they begin skimming through magazines looking for words they want to use or fonts they like, they will lose precious time and muddy the process.

I've also found that the students often incorporate the illustrations or photographs used in the article into their poems in some way. In the past I've had students glue the poem to the photo or use pieces of the art as decoration. The resulting found poem is as much visual art as it is creative writing, and most students seem to find this combination of craft very satisfying.

For a variation on this exercise, I also show the students *A humument* by Tom Phillips. Phillips has spent the better part of his career transforming a Victorian novel and finding poetry within its pages. The poet Austin Kleon has done this more recently with the *New York Times* and a

Sharpie, in his *Newspaper blackout*. He calls his technique 'newspaper blackout' because he eliminates all the words he doesn't need for his poems by blacking them out. Not as creative and colorful as *The humument*, the simplicity of his approach certainly appeals to some students.

Finding the poetry in the piece of writing comes easier to some than others. Don't be surprised if a few students create several poems.

The objective

For me, the objective of this exercise is to get people who don't consider themselves poets or those who feel uncomfortable about writing a poem to think about words and language. They begin to think poetically almost by accident. If I asked them to write a poem for homework, I suspect there would be much stress and many false starts. I am certain that the poems I would get would not be as experimental and playful as the ones created in class. In the past, I've received poems on everything from the National Football League to 'going commando'.

By limiting the pool of words they can draw from, I am encouraging them to hone in on the language before them as well as how the words look on the page. In a strange way, the limitations appear to liberate the writing.

Contributor: Colleen Kearney Rich

My parents named me Colleen because it is an Irish word meaning 'girl' and went very well with the Irish last name Kearney. I live in Fairfax, Virginia. Although I spend the bulk of my time writing magazine features for fun and profit, I also have two novels in need of revision. Stephen King's *On writing* is a book I often recommend. When not writing, I am usually attending a sports event for one of my three children. I can't help you with your taxes or Excel spreadsheets. If I didn't tell you, you would never know that I'm afraid of heights.

46

30/30 projects: developing a daily writing habit

Introduction
A 30/30 project is one where students write thirty poems in thirty days. Each day, they post their poems on an online class forum where they can also read the work of other students. I like to set up the project during April, the USA's National Poetry Month, or November, National Novel Writing Month, so students can tap into the creative energy of the larger writing community.

Students will find themselves entering a groove of daily writing within the first week. They will scour their days for subjects, listen out for potential first lines, observe their worlds carefully.

The project can also be adapted for fiction courses.

The exercise
I use Blackboard to set up the 30/30 project, but any online platform that supports forums will work, as long as students can post poems and comments.

On Day 1, I post the rules:

30/30 RULES
The rules are simple, young warriors:
1 poem/day for one month. Midnight marks a day.
Minimum 8 lines.
Any subject. Any form. Or no form.
Paste your poems into your post (no attachments).
BRING IT ON!

Each day gets its own forum. Each student creates a thread within the forum for his/her poem. I recommend that students use the titles of their poems as thread titles so others may find, at a glance, all of the authors and poems on a given day.

COMMENTS

For the first few days, it's important that the lecturer responds to each post. This creates momentum around the project and encourages students to pay regular attention to the discussion board. But set parameters for yourself. I announce to my students that I will read all their poems, but that I will also take some days off from commenting. However, each day I post and email a general comment that deals with the poems collectively rather than individually.

The best comments tend to be brief, encouraging, playful, specific, and generative: 'Whoa, you've raised your game in the last few days! In an otherwise tidy poem, the slant rhyme of *lust/gorgeous* is a welcome musical subtlety. Don't you think so?'

Remember the point of the 30/30 project is to develop a sustainable writing practice, so try not to get hung up on fixing the poems. Revision happens later in the semester or in a different forum, perhaps in face-to-face workshops. That said, a student may occasionally post a revised version of his/her poems but this is not a substitute for producing a new poem for that day.

HANDLING BURNOUT

There is a distinct rhythm to 30/30 projects. Students embark upon the first week enthusiastically, then some fall out during the middle weeks, then they all get a shot of adrenaline during the last week. As moderator, I also act as a cheerleader, and supply lots of *rah-rah* energy online and in class.

Prompts can work miracles during the middle part of the month. During one week, I suggest that students write in the style of other students. Each day, I announce a different student-poet, identify his/her stylistic strengths, point the class to a representative post, and invite interested students to imitate that style. Or, I might direct students to their own past poems for starting points. Ideally, students should keep an extra poem or two in their back pockets so they're prepared for a case of writer's block, illness, or busy periods.

EVALUATION

The project is worth a hefty portion of a student's final grade. You could choose to be very scientific with this exercise. Perhaps, each missed day warrants a five point penalty.

In general, I give high credit to students who complete the project according to the rules and schedule. That is the most important criterion. But, of course, a student who repeatedly produces eight casual lines will receive a lower grade than one who consistently produces thoughtful, high quality poems.

AN ADDITIONAL INCENTIVE

Students love it when you do this project with them. Simply knowing that you share their frustrations during week 3, for example, tightens the supportive nature of the community. The rules must be the same for you as for the students. No special privileges.

The objective

PRODUCING POEMS

The main purpose of the 30/30 project is to produce poems, quality being secondary to production, and to develop a habit of writing every day. Facilitated by technology, I find that students achieve more by practising and reading the work of other students than from a month's worth of lectures on poetic technique.

READING

The project makes it easy for students to read poetry. In my nightly comments, I link to model poems by established poets or to online literary journals. Without realising it, some students read more poetry in this month than they have in their entire undergraduate careers. They don't complain about oversaturation because their reading is quickly converted into poems of their own.

AN ALTERNATIVE TO WORKSHOPPING

A 30/30 can act as an alternative to workshopping. Although its main purpose is not to revise poems but to produce them, suggestions for improvement are inevitable during the month. This new space is a supplement to in-class meetings. It is relaxed, convenient, self-indexing, and traceable, since a student's body of work accumulates over the month.

USING NEW MEDIA TO BUILD COMMUNITY

Students appreciate that the project makes use of their considerable technological savvy. A 30/30 combines the intimacy of a traditional poetry class with the feeling of social media and the academic rigour of a science fair project. Technology is the vehicle to create a more intricate level of community beyond the classroom.

Each student will adapt the project according to his/her proclivities. Some will receive instant forum updates on their smart phones and keep the discussion board aflame with activity well into the early morning hours. Others will set up a regular time each day to post and respond to posts.

Contributor: Ian Williams
There are other Ian Williamses online – a British comedian, an American football player, an Australian computer scientist – but I am the one who lives at http://www. ianwilliams.ca. The *.ca* stands for Canada, which is where I'm from, although I'm currently an English professor in Massachusetts. I write poetry and fiction about you and you and maybe you over there. I recommend Kim Addonizio's *Ordinary genius*. I can't tell you anything about splashy Romantic ballets. All right, fine, I can tell you more than you care to know.

47

Using guided walks in creative writing: wandering, observing, describing

Introduction
In order for students to sharpen their descriptive powers, it is often effective to take a class outside for a walk instead of remaining in a classroom setting. By making brief stops and allowing students to range and explore by themselves, you can give them opportunities to record their perceptions in small notes and sketches. This process is akin to brainstorming as it allows students to scavenge the natural world and built environment for ideas, and may include literally collecting small objects where it is appropriate.

When students return to the classroom, they can be encouraged to use their journal-like entries as starting points to generate poems, stories, or essays. This exercise has wide applications and can be tailored to the time restrictions and needs of almost any writing class, whether elementary or advanced.

The exercise
It is important to notify students ahead of time that they will be walking outside during class and that they should wear suitable clothing. Before heading outside, provide students with a few examples of physical objects that they may encounter, bringing them into the classroom if possible. Objects could be as commonplace as a leaf, a small stone, or a crumpled soda can. Guide students in

generating short descriptions of these objects in the form of a few sentence fragments. Ask them to focus on recording details and minutia such as the network of veins on a leaf or the particular spikes, whorls, and spirals on a seashell: the more specific their notes are, the more useful the exercise will be in sharpening their powers of description. As you discuss students' descriptions, encourage free-writing and emphasise that their responses do not have to be polished, but are expected to take the form of telegraphic jottings or journal entries. Also, before venturing outside, make sure you clearly circumscribe the boundaries in which students are allowed to wander, as well as explaining any other rules that you wish them to follow.

Outside, students should range over the chosen terrain on their own or in pairs, taking notes on different objects. The lecturer's role at this point is to encourage students to strike a balance between writing and observing since it's easy for them to become preoccupied with one or the other. It can help to ask them to produce a full page of notes on at least six different objects, for example, in order to keep them focused. In addition, pointing out interesting natural phenomena or artefacts for the more reluctant students can help them get started.

Upon reconvening in class or as a group outside, have students share some of their findings. During discussion, suggest ways that the students' notes could be developed into poems, used as elements of a story setting, or incorporated into a personal essay. For example, a poem could use a description of a particular object as an extended metaphor or it could be based on the encounter of several objects that shaped the experience of the walk. I often give a follow-up or homework assignment to complete a draft of a piece of creative writing based on the notes that the student took during the walk, which is taken through the workshop process.

VARIATIONS

In addition to writing short descriptions during their walk, try suggesting that the students collect small objects or make sketches and drawings. The benefit to doing so is that some students will write more evocative descriptions when they have time to contemplate objects later instead of feeling hurried to jot down notes on the spot. However, the drawback to this is that students may write less during class if they are encouraged to sketch or collect, and you'll need to get them to use extreme discretion when deciding which objects they remove from the habitat.

I have used this exercise in traditional creative writing classes, as well as adapting it for classes on playwriting, journal writing, and architectural writing. In the playwriting class, students were instructed to scout for site-specific environments in which to locate their plays and performances. In the journal writing class, although the notes students took on their walks were later revised, the act of journaling was promoted as an end in itself, and journals and notebooks viewed as legitimate creative writing genres in their own right. In the architectural writing class, the urban instead of natural world was the focus of our excursions, with students instructed to observe different infrastructural networks and the ways that built spaces interact with their environments.

In fact, I have even done guided walks entirely indoors, having students take notes on the designed use of space versus how various users have repurposed the space, demarcations of public and private zones, or other overlooked features of a building. Using walks to inspire student writing can take place anywhere, whether your setting is urban, suburban, or rural.

The objective
This exercise achieves several objectives: it acts as a brainstorming activity to generate topics, it helps strengthen students' imagery and powers of description, and it requires students to revise their initial work. By focusing students' attention on the immediacy of the world around them, they have both a constraint on their subject matter and an impetus to write. Hopefully, students who closely observe the objects and conditions surrounding them will reflect this in the language they use: their imagery and details will become richer, more evocative, and more precise. Having students use a notebook to record their observations will emphasise the writing process; when students go back to their notebook for ideas, they will need to incorporate, revise, rearrange, rewrite, and discard their jottings as they work to craft a more finished piece. Finally, this exercise encourages students to employ a notebook in their daily lives, making writing a more habitual practice.

Contributor: Will Cordeiro
My name is William J. Cordeiro. My family called me 'B.J.' as a child, and I was nicknamed 'Fake' on my college cross-country team. I lived in Brooklyn for several years but now reside in upstate New York. I write in all creative genres, as well as engaging in journalism and academic research. I recommend that you read David Mamet's *Three uses of the knife*. Ask me if you want to learn about

eighteenth-century topiary gardens. I can't help you cook *canard à la rouennaise* any. If I didn't tell you, you'd never know I once dressed up as an armadillo for Halloween.

48

Researching for the fiction writer

Introduction
There is a certain level of authenticity – namely, in the science – in Margaret Atwood's speculative novel *Oryx and Crake*. Atwood makes plain on her acknowledgement page the research that has lent to that believability in the novel. I present my students, who may feel limited in subject matter, with this page and similar pages from other books, to show that it is perfectly acceptable to write from research in fiction writing.

I created the following exercise to help students learn how research can work in fiction writing. It invites them to acquire information through research in order to write about topics they do not know much about. Of course, their personal experiences may lend to their stories, but research can supply details that they would not have known without it.

This should be considered a homework assignment, as students have to actually research various topics in order to complete it. Because I treat this assignment as an exercise, I do not ask my students to turn in a completed story, but at least two pages of either an excerpt of a story or a draft of a short-short.

The exercise
I use the following in a handout, but you could change this to suit any fiction class.

Research project

Research can play an important role in fiction. While some writers may start from the background of an exotic job or travel to exciting places, it's not unusual to feel lacking in the area of broad experience. This should not keep anyone from writing about workers being trapped down in a coal mine or American Egyptologists stuck in Cairo during the January 25 Revolution.

For this assignment, please research at least two potential elements of a story, such as a profession or a setting, and incorporate them into a piece of fiction. The story does not have to be complete, but it should be at least 600 words long (about two pages).

METHOD

1. Pick a specific profession – not a writer and preferably something unfamiliar to you.
2. Pick one more element. It can be a place, a historical event, a religion, whatever. This is up to you.
3. Research the profession and the other element using any research method you like. You may start with Google, for instance, then end at the hospital – not as a patient(!), shadowing a phlebotomist or a paediatric nurse. Use the telephone, the library, the zoo, or any resource you think would be successful. Just do some fancy foot, or finger, or eye work and get your research done!
4. Begin a short story, or write a short-short, incorporating some of what you have learned. Your main character should probably work in whatever profession you looked up, or someone close to your main character should have that job.

Do not let the research restrict you, but rather, let it inform your work. For instance, you do not have to go over the procedures a phlebotomist must take before drawing blood, but that procedural process may influence her behaviour at a dinner party.

I do not ask my students to prove their research with a bibliography, but I ask each one to tell the class how s/he completed the research leg of the assignment with details of shadowing, searching the Internet, interviewing, or whichever method was used.

Many students go on to polish these exercises into completed short-shorts or short stories featuring a myriad of occupations and places. Some of my favourite finished projects included a character who was a hobby whiskey distiller, a tow truck driver who removed vehicles from fatal accidents, and a cake designer for a royal wedding.

The objective

With this assignment, students should learn that research is an essential feature in fiction writing, and can be invited to look at the acknowledgement pages of books such as *Oryx and Crake*, as mentioned above, or Sara Gruen's *Water for elephants*.

Seeing published writers' use of research encourages students to take the task seriously.

Students, too, should feel and be empowered to write about topics outside of their level of expertise. They should leave the assignment ready to learn what they do not know through various kinds of research.

Contributor : DeMisty D. Bellinger

My name is DeMisty Dawn Bellinger. My mother wanted to name me Defogelant and my father, mercifully, liked Misty. I remained nameless for a day, then they compromised. I live in Nebraska, which is in the middle of the USA. I write realistic fiction that varies between modern, post-modern, and experimental. I recommend that you read *How fiction works* by James Wood. Ask me if you need information on raising twins. I can't help you with decorating your home. You'd never have known if I hadn't told you that I really dig the Pixies and all of Frank Black's incarnations.

49

Writing with the masters:
finding creativity in copying

Introduction

I have always believed that good writers are probably all good readers and that creative writing students can learn from the established literary greats. After all, before one can draw from his own well of creativity, it is helpful to ensure that it is teeming with possibilities. By not only examining canonical works but by also including pieces of them in a new, original piece of writing, students can gain a much fuller appreciation of the true power and infinite potential of the written word.

This activity is one I use to encourage students to experiment with the vast possibilities inherent in working with genres and styles that might not come naturally to them; ideally, this will help them explore their options as they refine their own voices.

The exercise

The exercise was inspired by Valdimir Nabokov's posthumously published *The original of Laura*. However, it can easily be adapted to other authors and other works.

NABOKOV BACKGROUND

Vladimir Nabokov (1899–1977) was arguably one of the twentieth-century's most gifted prose stylists, and the manner in which he composed his masterpieces is especially unusual. Nabokov first penned all of his stories on index cards, and his final, incomplete, novel contains perforated facsimiles of every card. Each a paragraph or two in length, some contain fully realised and brilliantly portrayed scenes while others begin and end mid-thought.

Using Nabokov

Because of the nature of the book itself, *The original of Laura* is a perfect choice to introduce this exercise. All you need to be willing to do is to purchase one copy of the book and then punch out the perforated cards.

Distribute one of the cards with Nabokov's words on it to each of your students. Instruct them to incorporate whatever appears on the card into their own, unique story. Nabokov's words can be used at the beginning, middle, or end of the students' work; the purpose is simply to have students creatively conclude a unified story that has already been started. In fact, while I typically do not advocate writing under duress, I've found this assignment has proven most productive when it is given in class and students are given a time limit – the amount of time depends on the length of the work you wish them to produce. The primary goal of this activity is to just get students writing.

I find this exercise to be extremely useful in the early weeks of a creative writing class because it induces students to actually produce prose while eliminating the difficulties of getting started; after all, students are essentially beginning *in media res*. Further, having students begin with another's words eases the self-consciousness of sharing, perhaps for the first time, their own voice with another reader. As their stories will, at the most basic level, germinate from another's work the fear and self-consciousness of writing anything too personally revealing vanish. Most importantly, I find that students are often surprised at what they are able to create if they don't have time to over-think it.

NON-NABOKOV VARIATIONS

Because of the ease of using the 'pre-packaged' perforated index cards, *Laura* lends itself so readily to this exercise. However, this activity is easily adaptable to other works and other authors. With other books, it is merely a matter of selecting a few paragraphs to distribute. Choosing different types of passages (e.g. descriptive, moving, humorous, dialogue-heavy, etc.) will further advance students' creative range.

Contrasting Nabokov's enchanting, yet verbose style with Hemingway's verbal economy works well and having students ape them both will help them realise the stark contrasts in great literature. Sandra Cisneros's *The house on Mango Street* is an exemplar of richly precise figurative language that students would do well to emulate, and anything by Joyce or Woolf can be used for a real challenge. The point of this exercise, though, is not to allow students to see it as a challenge, but rather to encourage them to expand their own repertoires and step outside of their comfort zones, thereby stimulating true creativity.

Once students have completed their drafts, I like to have them take turns reading aloud, first the text they were given and then what they created from it. Even though they all began working with the style of one author, their finished products clearly reveal the true voice of each individual. Thus, by beginning with copied material, each student can begin to discover his own, unique voice.

For students, the more styles of writing they are exposed to, the more possibilities they will see for their own writing. For lecturers, hopefully you will enjoy perusing some of your favourite classics for paragraphs to lift for this exercise.

The objective

Ultimately, this assignment is designed to benefit students in two ways. First, it helps them overcome what for many is the most difficult part of the writing process: getting started. I have found that nothing is more intimidating to a burgeoning author than the glaring whiteness of a blank Word document. With this exercise, the imposing task of creating something from nothing is eliminated because the students are given text to start with.

Additionally, having young writers start with someone else's words enables them to find and/or refine their own voice, while pushing them outside of their established comfort zones leads them to discover techniques that they otherwise never would have. In the short term, this will provide them with an immediate taste – and distaste – for certain stylistic flourishes. In the long term, they will have an even deeper well to draw from as their own writing continues to develop and, perhaps, evolve from the influence of the masters.

Contributor: Adam Robert Floridia

I use my full name to show my initials spell 'ARF', which fits since I love dogs. I enjoy cavorting with my chocolate lab, Scout (named after my favourite character), in Meriden, Connecticut, a small city in a small state in the big USA. I generally just write boring scholarly stuff for obscure literary journals. However, I'm expanding my creative aptitude and recommend *The way we write*, edited by Barbara Baker. Don't come to me for any handiwork, but ask me all about Kurt Vonnegut. If I didn't tell you, you'd never know I have an extremely childish sense of humour.

50

Describing with feeling: evoking style, tone and emotion in script scene directions

Introduction

It's commonly perceived that a script is a blueprint: a mere 'map' towards making the final product, whether for screen, stage or radio. Unlike prose and poetry, the writing on the page is only a part of the product's realisation, not the product itself.

One problem with this idea is that some people therefore think a script doesn't have to have any style to it; it should just read as a simple outline. On the contrary, a script has as much work to do on the page as it does in performance. After all, a script has to be read as a story, as a text in itself, before it can then be commissioned for production.

This exercise is thus designed to encourage students to write well-crafted, engaging scene directions that mirror the style, tone and emotion of the story they envision beyond the script page.

The exercise

Students are asked to take a scene from their script, preferably between one and two pages long, and think about the context in which it sits. For example, what kind of drama is being written? What genre does the drama fit? What has happened before this scene? What happens after this scene? How do they want their audience to feel when watching or listening to the drama? How do they want their audience to feel when watching or listening to this scene?

Once the context has been considered, work can begin on honing the scene to make it leap from the page. Note the importance of knowing a lot about the *feeling* of the piece; the feeling as in the genre (emotional responses to unfolding action), and the feeling as in thematic values (what the audience takes away with them). This is really important when writing scene directions because, above all, a writer is trying to elicit a strong connection between the audience and the text; they are trying to make the audience *feel* the drama.

The scene can now be analysed and the scene directions enhanced by working through the following four areas: pace; action; visual landscape; layout.

PACE

We talk a lot about pace when writing drama, but this usually refers to the whole drama rather than specific scenes. We often talk about using visual sequences, juxtaposing story threads, etc. Writing scenes is also about writing pace, and using pace to mirror the feelings anticipated of the audience.

For example, consider the difference between 'Mary is sitting in her living room, looking at the clock intermittently, waiting for Simon to return home' and 'Mary sits. And sits. The clock ticks. She looks up, intermittently, waiting.' Although both scene directions give exactly the same information, the former is rather bland and detached from the character of Mary, whilst the latter is more evocative of the painful time that Mary is enduring as she waits for Simon. Quite simply, writing the direction in beats that mirror the character's inner turmoil gives a stronger sense of the how the scene's pace would be played out when eventually produced.

Students should be asked to identify passages of scene description and find ways of fine-tuning the wording to more accurately reflect what's going on in the scene. If there's time, they would benefit from working with peers who could evaluate the effectiveness of their descriptions. Reading aloud is a useful technique for this.

ACTION

A simple exercise in evaluating how verbs are used can really enhance the power of a scene. Here, the intention is to create a more accurate sense of how a character does something, and by association, also create a stronger sense of the visual composition of a scene.

Students should highlight all of the verbs used in their scene descriptions, and, thinking again about the context, consider whether more suitable ones would create a stronger understanding of the scene. For example, the difference between 'Marco walks', 'Marco strides', 'Marco saunters' and 'Marco minces' is one of more than semantics. The verbs here all relate to the same action, but very specifically define his character in different ways. Similarly, 'Emma laughs' tells us nothing compared to 'Emma cackles', 'Emma giggles' or 'Emma sneers'.

Encourage students to really think about their characters' personalities and intentions when writing lines of action for them.

VISUAL LANDSCAPE

Although specific directorial shots are best avoided (close-ups, pans, etc.), writers can allude to this by careful scene descriptions that evoke a sense of the visual landscape. In this way, students should be encouraged to compose the screen as a director would, through subtle detail.

Ask students to take a section of their scene where they would envisage a specific set of camera angles, and ask them to evoke this through description that focuses the reader's mind on the visual landscape.

For example, if a horror requires a close-up of a knife blade very close to the victim's face, then an expression like 'The blade reflects in the pupils of her eyes' clearly suggests this. Similarly, 'The horses gallop across the plain, the sun sinking behind them' suggests a long, wide shot that uses the whole frame.

Not all screen directions will need this amount of detail, of course, but consciously thinking in directorial terms will positively enhance the visuality of a scene.

LAYOUT

Finally, the layout of scene descriptions can have an impact upon how they are read and thus experienced. The general rule-of-thumb is that a direction should run for no more than four lines before a paragraph break is inserted, but in many cases it can be less than this. It's a useful exercise to look at the layout of a poem and ask students to consider why the text is broken up in such a way, and then translate those ideas into scene directions.

Ask students to play around with their scene direction layout, first of all making each one (each paragraph) as short as possible, and then each one as long as possible. Through reading the directions aloud, with a pause in between each paragraph, ask them to consider how the style, tone and emotion changes in each scenario. Does one suit the needs of the scene better? Is one more appealing than the other? What happens when there is a combination of both?

The objective

This exercise should really encourage students to hone in on their scenes and spend quality time rewriting their material. Rather than assuming that a scene just works, it asks students to question if the scene really does work, and encourages them to play around with alternatives that might actually make better writing.

From the lecturer's point-of-view, the exercise is also designed to enhance the reading experience of students' scripts, so much so that hopefully marking will become less of a burden!

Contributor: Craig Batty

My name is Craig Batty. I write screenplays and books about screenwriting, and also work as a script consultant on other people's screenplays. I recommend *The writer's journey: mythic structure for writers* by Christopher Vogler. When I'm not writing, I like to spend time in public places such as cafés, restaurants and the leisure centre. Ask me if you need information on soap operas and money-saving deals. I can't help you with football. You'd never have known if I hadn't told you that I have a secret desire to be an airline pilot.

Afterword

Writing outside the book

The most obvious way to get the best from this book is to use the thematic index to search for specific subjects and techniques. It offers connections between the exercises to help you create or refresh a series of class outlines or a scheme of work. The book is also designed to fit easily into a bag as a stand-by on days when inspiration fails you or you're asked to cover someone else's class. The e-book option broadens its accessibility – one way or the other, you can have it on hand.

However, in the interests of a creative approach, there are several additional ways to add value to its practicality:

1. Use the author bios as a starting point for a workshop in character study or give each student just one as the basis for a short story.

2. Try one exercise with different groups of students – let their responses spin it off in new directions then use those for future groups.

3. Choose three exercises at random, then make one activity by combining them. Or, instead of making this combination yourself, ask your students to do it, working in small groups. Then ask each group to lead part of the next session to try out the activity they have devised.

4. Use the title/sub-title of an exercise for a ten-minute free-writing session.

5. Dip into the book at random and commit to using whichever exercise you arrive at, even if that will shake your group up a little. After they've done it, discuss how using a change of direction can refresh the overall focus of the course.

Creative eclecticism was the starting point for this book, using the connection of writing in higher education to draw together contributors from different countries, writing traditions and personal backgrounds. By using that eclecticism with our own students, we can look for connections outside the familiar. The old advice to write what we know then ceases to be a safety net and becomes a springboard.

Finally, while there is plenty of material here to keep you and your students busy, it's inevitable that there will be exercises that don't immediately seem useful – you could use those first.

ELAINE WALKER

Bibliography

Kathleen Adams, *Journal to the self: twenty-two paths to personal growth* (New York: Grand Central Publishing, 1990).

Kathleen Adams, *The way of the journal: a journal therapy workbook for healing* (Brooklandville: The Sidran Press, 1998).

Kim Addonizio, *Ordinary genius: a guide for the poet within* (New York: Norton, 2009).

Naomi Adler, *The Barefoot book of animal tales* (Bath: Barefoot Books, 1996).

Margaret Atwood, *Oryx and Crake* (New York: Nan A. Talese, 2003).

Barbara Baker (ed.), *The way we write* (London: Continuum, 2007).

M.M. Bakhtin, *Problems of Dostoevsky's poetics* (Minneapolis: University of Minnesota Press, 1984).

J.G. Ballard, *Drought* (London: Penguin, 1977).

Charles Baxter, *The art of subtext: beyond plot* (St. Paul: Gray Wolf Press, 2007).

Samuel Beckett, *Collected shorter plays* (New York: Grove Press, 1984).

Anne Bernays and Pamela Painter, *What if?: writing exercises for fiction writers* (New York: HarperCollins, 1990).

Laura Berk, *Child development* (Boston: Allyn & Bacon, 2003).

Dorothea Brande, *Becoming a writer* (London: Macmillan, 1996).

Charlotte Brontë, *Jane Eyre* (London: Penguin Classics, 2009).

Emily Brontë, *Wuthering Heights* (London: Penguin Classics, 2009).

Arthur Brooke, *The tragicall historye of Romeus and Iuliet,* (London, 1562).

Janet Burroway and Elizabeth Stuckey-French, *Writing fiction: a guide to narrative craft* (London: Longman, 2006).

Truman Capote, *Breakfast at Tiffany's* (London: Penguin Essentials, 2011).

Sandra Cisneros, *The house on Mango Street* (New York: Vintage, 1991).

Arthur Conan Doyle, *The hound of the Baskervilles* (London: Penguin Classics, 2004).

Helen Corner and Lee Weatherly, *Write a blockbuster and get it published* (London: Teach Yourself @ Hodder Headline, 2010).

David Crystal, *Making sense of grammar* (Harlow: Pearson Longman, 2004).

David Crystal, *Rediscover grammar* (Harlow: Pearson Longman, 2004).

A. Danchev (ed.), *100 artists' manifestos: from the Futurists to the Stuckists* (London: Penguin Modern Classics, 2011).

Bei Dao, *The rose of time: new and selected poems* (New York: New Directions, 2009).

Paul Dawson, *Creative writing and the new humanities* (Oxford: Routledge, 2005).

Carol Ann Duffy, *Mean time* (Vancouver: Anvil Press, 1993).

George Eliot, *Mill on the Floss* (London: Penguin Classics, 1980).

David Elkind, *Children and adolescents: interpretive essays on Piaget* (Oxford: Oxford University Press, 1981).

Donna Farhi, *Bringing yoga to life* (New York: HarperCollins, 2005).

Katie Ford, *Deposition* (St Paul: Graywolf Press, 2004).

Kate Grenville, *The writing book* (Sydney: Allen & Unwin, 1995).

Sara Gruen, *Water for elephants* (New York: Algonquin Books of Chapel Hill, 2006).

Sara Haslam and Derek Neale, *Life writing* (Abingdon: Routledge, 2009).

David Hayman, David Michaelis, George Plimpton and Richard Rhodes (eds.), 'The art of fiction no. 64: Kurt Vonnegut', *Paris Review* 69: spring 1977.

Ernest Hemingway, *The old man and the sea* (London: Vintage Classics, 2000).

Eric Henderson and Geoff Hancock, *Short fiction and critical contexts: a compact reader* (Oxford: Oxford University Press, 2010).

Ted Hughes, *Poetry in the making* (London: Faber and Faber, 1967).

Celia Hunt and Fiona Sampson, *Writing: self and reflexivity* (London: Palgrave Macmillan, 2005).

Franz Kafka, *Metamorphosis and other stories* (London: Penguin Modern Classics, 2007).

Stephen King, *On writing: a memoir of the craft* (London: New English Library, 2007).

Brian Kiteley, *The 3 a.m. epiphany: uncommon writing exercises that transform your fiction* (Cincinnati: Writer's Digest Books, 2005).

Barbara Kingsolver, *The poisonwood bible* (New York: Harper Flamingo, 1998).

Austin Kleon, *Newspaper blackout* (New York: Harper Perennial, 2010).

Kenneth Koch, *Making your own days: the pleasures of reading and writing poetry* (New York: Simon & Schuster, 1999).

Anne Lamott, *Bird by bird: instructions on life and writing* (New York: Pantheon Books, 1994).

Priscilla Long, *The writer's portable mentor* (Seattle: Wallingford Press, 2010).

David Mamet, *Three uses of the knife: on the uses and purposes of drama* (New York: Vintage, 2000).

Adrian May, *Myth and creative writing: the self-renewing song* (Harlow: Longman 2011).

Steve May, *Doing creative writing* (London: Routledge, 2007).

China Miéville, *Rejectamentalist* (http://chinamieville. net/).

Andrew Melrose, *Write for children* (London: Routledge, 2002).

Steven Millhauser, *The knife thrower, and other stories* (NY: Random House, 1998).

Michel de Montaigne, *Les essais*, vol. 1 (Paris: Chez Michel Sonnius, 1595).

Dinty W. Moore, *Crafting the personal essay: a guide for writing and publishing creative non-fiction* (Fairfield OH: Writer's Digest, 2010).

Valdimir Nabokov, *The Original of Laura* (New York: Knopf, 2009).

Jenny Newman, Edmund Cusick and Aileen La Tourette (eds.), *The writer's workbook* (London: Arnold, 2004).

Tom Phillips, *A humument* (London: Thames & Hudson, 2005).

Ovid, *Metamorphoses*, trans. Mary M. Innes (Harmondsworth: Penguin, 1955).

Ruth Padel, *52 ways of looking at a poem* (London: Vintage, 2004).

Grace Paley, *Begin again: collected poems* (New York: Farrar, Straus and Giroux, 2001).

Suzan-Lori Parks, *365 days/365 plays* (New York: Theatre Communications Group, 2006).

George Plimpton (ed.), *Playwrights at work: the Paris Review interviews* (London: Harvill Press, 2000).

Francine Prose, *Reading like a writer* (New York: Harper Perennial, 2006).

Purdue Online Writing Lab (http://owl.english.purdue. edu/owl/section/1/5/, accessed 3 April 2011).

Raymond Queneau, *Exercises in style*, trans. Barbara Wright (London: Gaberbocchus Press, 1958).

Burton Raffel, *How to read a poem* (New York: New American Library, 1984).

A. Siebold and H. Pitlor (eds.), *The best American short stories 2009* (New York: Mariner Books, 2009).

William Shakespeare, *An excellent conceited tragedie of Romeo and Iuliet* (London, 1597).

Ali Smith, *The accidental* (London: Hamish Hamilton, 2005).

Hazel Smith, *The writing experiment: strategies for innovative creative writing* (London: Allen & Unwin, 2005).

David Starkey, *Creative writing: four genres in brief* (Boston: Bedford, 2009).

Gertrude Stein, *Three lives* (New York: Penguin Books, 1990).

Sarah Stone and Ron Nyren, *Deepening fiction* (New York: Longman, 2004).

Mark Strand and Eavan Boland, *The making of a poem* (New York and London: Norton, 2001).

William Strunk Jr. and E.B. White, *The elements of style* (New York: Longman, 1999).

Todd Swift and Philip Norton (eds.) *Short fuse: the global anthology of new fusion poets* (New York: Rattapallax Press, 2002).

Dylan Thomas, *Collected poems* (London: Phoenix, 2000).

Edward Thomas, *Collected poems* (London: Faber, 2004).

The University of Ottawa Hypergrammar (http://www.writingcentre.uottawa.ca/hypergrammar/, accessed 3 April 2011).

Christopher Vogler, *The writer's journey: mythic structure for writers* (Studio City, CA: Michael Wiese Productions, 2007).

John Whitworth, *Writing poetry* (London, A&C Black, 2006).

James Wood, *How fiction works* (New York: Farrar, Straus and Giroux, 2008).

W. B. Yeats, *Collected poems* (Hertfordshire: Wordsworth Editions, 1994).

William Zinsser (ed.), *Inventing the truth: the art and craft of memoir* (Boston: Houghton Mifflin, 1998).

Thematic index

This book provides fifty ideas for teaching creative writing in universities and colleges. There are as many routes through its pages as there are readers. This section offers some ideas for navigation by picking out common themes and topics.

Numbers refer to exercises, not pages.

Characterisation
Character development and shaping plot, 6, 9, 10, 18, 31
Creating believable characters, 7, 26
Getting characters to interact, 9, 33
Using characters' desires and emotions, 18, 31

Developing skills
Breaking down barriers to writing poetry, 16, 28, 29, 35, 43, 45, 46
Exploring the potential in familiar things 2, 5, 21, 30, 47
Providing models and starting points 4, 10, 15, 16, 39, 44, 45, 49
Stimulating creativity and flow 7, 12, 14, 29, 35, 41, 43, 46

Developing writing practice
Awareness of reader/audience interpretation, 29, 36, 44, 50
Learning from other writers, 3, 4, 15, 17, 44, 39, 40, 49
Openness and flexibility, 11, 13, 24, 29
Purposeful writing: argument and persuasion, 11, 13
Researching for fiction and nonfiction, 13, 37, 47, 48
Self-critique 3, 24, 34
Self-discipline 39, 46

Exercise duration
One hour or less, 2, 8, 18, 21, 41
Up to two hours/one session, 5, 8, 12, 15, 18, 45
Two sessions, 26, 30, 35
Several weeks/sessions 3, 11, 17, 34

Fiction
Character, plot, setting 7, 9, 10, 15, 18, 31
Editing and redrafting 3, 8, 24, 25
Narrative mode 6, 23, 26, 33, 37, 40

Genre
Fiction
Fantasy, 7; Flash fiction, 8; For children, 27; Micro fiction, 8;
  Monologues, 10; Drama, 32, 38, 50; Short stories, 7, 8, 31,
  48; Suspense, 40; Young adult, 37

Non-fiction
Critical reflective essay, 34; Food writing, 21; Travel writing, 5

Poetry
Pantoum, 16; Performance poetry, 19, 28; Prose poem, 25;
  Sonnet, 16, 43

Song writing 42

Particularly suitable for ...
All stages, 10, 13, 15, 25, 29, 37, 47
Collaborative working, 1, 3, 9, 11, 12, 18, 28, 29, 36, 41
Confident writers, 11
Intermediate writers, 18
Introductions, 1, 8, 9, 20, 39
New groups, 1, 8, 9, 10, 20, 28, 35
New students, 7, 9, 14, 18, 20, 30, 39, 41
Online courses, 1, 20, 24, 39, 46
Towards the end of a course, 3
Undergraduates, 4, 5, 8, 28, 43, 46

Performance
Bringing plays and screenplays to life, 32, 38, 50
Poetry and prose out loud 19, 22, 28

Poetry
Listening to poetry to aid critiquing and editing skills, 19, 22
Considering rhythm in poetry and song, 22, 42
Practising ways of developing meaning, 25, 29, 36, 43

Point of view
Using free indirect style to gain narrative flexibility, 6
Using multiple view points for narrative enrichment and
    development, 33
Writing from opposing viewpoints, 13

Reading
Close reading to extend critical and self-reflexive skills, 3, 4, 39
Looking at techniques authors use in order to inform students'
    writing, 3, 4, 15, 17, 27, 39, 40, 44, 49

Setting and context
Using senses, memories or observations, 2, 5, 12, 21, 30, 47
Use of place, 15

Structure
Creating structure from bottom up: words, sentences and
    paragraphs, 4, 17, 40
Creating structure in short stories, 8, 31

Students' common needs
Confidence building and icebreakers, 1, 9, 10, 11, 20, 28, 35,
    39, 41
Gaining critical and reflexive skills, 3, 11, 12, 24, 29, 35
Working with other students, 1, 3, 9, 11, 28, 29, 35, 41
Writing the critical reflective essay, 34

Virtual learning
Developing and editing texts in a virtual space, 20, 24, 39, 46
Ice breakers online 1, 20, 39

Voice
Using monologues to discuss perceptions and the credibility of
  voice, 10
Using second person perspective in prose, 23
Writing for children, 26
Writing for young adults, 37
See also **Point of view**